A Clinician's Guide to
Gender Identity and Body Image

A Clinician's Guide to Gender Identity and Body Image

Practical Support for Working with Transgender and Gender-Expansive Clients

Heidi Dalzell, PsyD, CEDS
and Kayti Protos, MSW, LCSW

Jessica Kingsley Publishers
London and Philadelphia

First published in 2020
by Jessica Kingsley Publishers
73 Collier Street
London N1 9BE, UK
and
400 Market Street, Suite 400
Philadelphia, PA 19106, USA

www.jkp.com

Library of Congress Cataloging in Publication Data
Names: Dalzell, Heidi, author. | Protos, Kayti, author.
Title: A clinician's guide to gender identity and body image : practical
  support for working with transgender and gender-expansive clients / Heidi
  Dalzell and Kayti Protos.
Description: London ; Philadelphia : Jessica Kingsley Publishers, 2020. |
  Includes bibliographical references.
Identifiers: LCCN 2019004547 | ISBN 9781785928307
Subjects: | MESH: Sexual and Gender Minorities--psychology | Health Services
  for Transgender Persons | Culturally Competent Care | Gender Identity |
  Body Image--psychology | Feeding and Eating Disorders--therapy
Classification: LCC RA564.9.T73 | NLM WM 617 | DDC 362.1086/6-
-dc23 LC record available at https://lccn.loc.gov/2019004547

British Library Cataloguing in Publication Data
A CIP catalogue record for this book is available from the British Library

ISBN 978 1 78592 830 7
eISBN 978 1 78450 971 2

Printed and bound by CPI Group (UK) Ltd, Croydon, CR0 4YY

Acknowledgments

F. Scott Fitzgerald said that "all good writing is swimming under water and holding your breath." We have had a number of people help us gently float to the surface. First and foremost, thank you to Michael Dalzell. As a life partner to one of us and a friend to the other, he tirelessly read chapter after chapter, providing feedback about topics he probably never imagined he'd be learning about. As an ally himself, as well as a talented writer, his editing and feedback were invaluable throughout this process.

Another important influence was our colleague, and frequent co-presenter Dr. Stacy Hunt, who helped us to develop many of the ideas you will see described in the book. We'd especially like to credit her for helping us to think about approaches to changing the body as akin to corrective surgery. She is also a loving mom to children who can always feel safe exploring gender, as well as a gifted therapist.

To all the staff at the Bucks LGBT Center, thank you for doing this important work with grace and acceptance.

We have also had the support of several influential professionals. Thank you to Sean Baker, a true pioneer in working with LGBT clients. His encouragement in our power as allies was influential. Similarly, thank you to Myles Marcotte, a budding therapist who courageously shared his own journey.

Our intern, Kelsey Fuller, was invaluable in helping to gather programs for our Resource Guide, as well as other behind-the-scenes tasks.

Last, but not least, thanks to our clients and their families, who have been brave, dignified, and remarkable in sharing their gender journeys with us.

Contents

Introduction

I hate my body. I hate the shape of my face. I was misgendered today at work. At school. At home. By my friend. By my manager. By my mom. By my teachers. By complete strangers. I hate the first day of school. Teachers never get it right. I skipped school again today. That guy pushed me down the stairs again. I wish I had hips like the cisgender girls in my school. I wish I had their hormones. I wish I had facial hair. I wish I was smaller. Bigger. Curvier. Stronger. Taller. I hate my voice. I hate my curves. I hate how big my hands and feet are. I hate going into stores and being unable to find clothes that fit me. I hate how ridiculously gendered stores and clothing are. Why is everything about gender? Where do I fit? No one understands.

Many of the clients we see in our therapy practice seek help with eating disorders, and almost all struggle with body image. Over the last few years, there has been an increase in the number of clients who identify as transgender or gender expansive. Some share their identities with us early in the therapeutic process, while others come out months or years later.

As more clients who were gender expansive entered our practice, we looked for research and best practices about the intersection of eating disorders and gender identity. There was only minimal information. Along with our colleague, Dr. Stacy Hunt, we sought to fill these gaps. This book shares stories of our transgender and gender-expansive clients, especially those who struggle with gender and body dysphoria and with eating disorders.

Fast forward a few months.

As Heidi reviewed her handwritten notes one last time, Kayti moved around the front of the conference room, taping signs with phrases like

"Body Dissociation/Hate" and "Body Acceptance" to any surface she could find. The room gradually began to fill as clinicians, educators, and medical professionals attended the first workshop in the professional track of the Philadelphia Trans Wellness Conference. We took a few breaths and began our workshop: Gender and Body Image Beyond the Binary: Working with Gender-Expansive and Transgender Clients. The room was filled to capacity with professionals seeking to support their clients who struggle with similar issues.

It is exciting to expand on the ideas generated from our workshop series and invite you to join us. What inspired you to pick up this book? What do you hope to gain from reading it?

One of our intentions is to encourage conversation about gender and body image beyond the binary. Both of us are cisgender but we are strong advocates and allies for working with body image and gender identity. Allyship is the process of providing active support for people of all gender identities and presentations. Allyship is an ongoing process of learning, respect, and understanding. As cis allies, we have privilege, including body privilege. We can use public restrooms without the threat of bullying or intimidation, our validity is not based on how well we pass, and we are not routinely asked what our "real" names are.

You will find many examples of cis privilege throughout this book. For information about being an ally of transgender and gender-expansive people, please see the National Center for Transgender Equality's article, *Supporting the Transgender People in Your Life: A Guide to Being a Good Ally* (2016). Being aware of the potential privileges (or lack thereof) that your identities bring to this conversation allows you to continue with an open mind.

Throughout the book, composite case examples are used to represent the voices of transgender and gender-expansive clients. Confidentiality is a fundamental principle of our profession, and identifying details have been changed and frequently combined across client situations to protect the privacy of individual clients and their families. All names are pseudonyms. Many individuals in the LGBTQ+ (lesbian, gay, bisexual, transgender, questioning and plus) community experience the difficulty of being "outed" by others, intentionally or unintentionally. This mandates an additional layer of protection for the clients represented in this book, and it is important to share their voices confidentially while maintaining the integrity of the clinical presentation.

HEIDI'S STORY

You may be asking yourself how does a cisgender woman come to co-author a book about working with transgender, gender-expansive, and nonbinary clients? Prior to the last decade, I would not have envisioned myself writing a book about helping people who are gender expansive negotiate body image. I did not know the meaning of words like nonbinary, gender expression, or cisgender. As a professional in the field of eating disorders for many years, I have always been passionate about body image—and yet I never stopped to consider how body image could differ for transgender people. If I did think about these questions, then, like many people, I grouped gender-expansive people within the entire LGBT spectrum.

About 15 years ago, I began seeing my first trans clients. They came to me primarily because my professional profile listed expertise in treating LGBT people. In retrospect, what I really meant was that I often treated gay, lesbian, and bisexual people, especially those with eating disorders. In fact, 15 years ago, there was still the belief that any man who walked through my door was gay or struggling with sexual orientation. Fortunately, times have changed.

The first trans folks I worked with trickled in slowly. It would generally go something like this. In our initial phone call, they would provide a vague reason for coming in, like "stress." In the initial session, we would talk for about 45 minutes when they dropped what they thought was a bombshell: "Dr. Dalzell, I'm not really here to talk about this. I actually feel more like a man [or woman] and I'm looking for support in sorting this out." In fact, the first time a client related some version of this, I was confused. I thought he was male, due to his outward presentation. He had been living as his non-assigned gender for many years, but was still struggling with deeply internalized transphobia and body hatred. He had limited sources of support, and his family had all but abandoned him. There were no handbooks to tell us how to proceed, and sources for consultation were limited. It often came down to remaining connected and compassionate, and mirroring my own acceptance of him. In subsequent therapies with other clients, I used my work with "Denny" as a template.

In my own family, gender norms were not an issue. While my daughter identifies as cisgender, she does not follow traditional gender norms in terms of interest or dress, preferring hockey jerseys and flannels to clothes from Forever 21. Some people would call this "gender nonconforming," but she does not label it this way. She came out as gay when she was a teen.

I respect and support this identity, and think she would agree that I have been an ally. I hope that I have always provided support in her choices.

Perhaps the client and experience that most cemented my interest in the intersection of body image and challenging the gender binary was a 14-year-old whom I will call Jade. With a past history of bulimia and present self-harm symptoms, Jade was a natural fit for my practice. After several months, Jade began to trust me and reached out to share a secret. In a letter I will describe more in Chapter 1, Jade revealed that his preferred name was Jared, and that he (his preferred pronoun) was questioning his gender. The letter ended with the plaintive words "I am a boy and it hurts." Working with Jared and his family, I learned a lot about the role of family support, how rigid religious boundaries can be traumatic, the importance of peers and supports, and other lessons that have been integrated into my work. Foremost, it helped me to understand more about body image and the connections between gender identity and eating disorders.

A simple definition of body image is "how people see themselves when they look in the mirror or when they picture themselves in their minds." When I think about this definition, there is a disconnect in many of my clients who have identified as gender expansive. For Jared, the external mirror showed an androgynous but more feminine image. In his mind's eye, Jared saw himself as a boy. He knew that most other people did not see him as a boy, and he was very sad about that. At times when he did pass as masculine, he felt more confident. When Jared was outed, misgendered, or told his presentation was "wrong," he punished his hated female body parts by cutting them. You will get to know Jared better in examples throughout the book.

Since that time, I have worked with many people and families who identify as gender expansive. I've partnered with Kayti, who shares a similar interest in eating disorders, body image, and working with gender identity. Kayti has the unique perspective of being a lesbian woman and understanding the struggles associated with being a member of the LGBT community. She also has a great sense of humor, which is essential to this work.

In our work within the eating disorder and trans healthcare communities, we have identified a lack of literature specific to body image in trans and gender-expansive people. In fact, Injustice at Every Turn, a recent large-scale research project about discrimination within the US transgender community, does not include any information about body image or eating disorders. In many ways, this is new ground. And while it may seem like this work should be done by members of the transgender community, there are not enough members to keep up with the needs. A wise colleague, Sean, told us "We need all the allies we can get." I hope that with the help of this book, you can also become an informed ally.

KAYTI'S STORY

My hands remained icicles, even as they rested deep within the fleece-lined pockets of my too-big Vanderbilt sweatshirt. I sat uncomfortably on the therapist's couch, trying not to touch the blonde-haired client sitting next to me. My underweight body curled even more tightly within itself. My body ached from the weight of both the meal we had just consumed together and that morning's conversation with a therapist on staff. *Please don't talk about your...identity...here, as you would make the other clients uncomfortable. My mind raced from one anxious thought to the next. Did that really happen? How many calories were in that meal? How many hours at the gym do I need to avoid gaining weight? Why do people think I'm a threat to others? Is there any way I can skip the snacks? I'm not even thinking about dating someone now; I'm barely able to take care of myself. How fast until I can get out of this room? Does that blonde girl know I'm gay? Don't think these thoughts. You're not allowed to think these thoughts. Pass the time, plan for tonight, skip dinner. You are in control. Why do therapists only talk about women's body image as it relates to the men? Do I even belong here? Smile and nod, then take control. You don't need any more food today. You don't need to nourish a body that is so wrong anyway.* As soon as the clock hands signaled the end of the partial-hospitalization day, I moved as quickly as possible out of the building while protecting my facade as calm-and-collected Kayti.

Oh my, here we go again. This gynecologist was nice enough in her pencil skirt and Southern twang, just like the handful of doctors before her. She smiled politely as she scanned my intake paperwork. She asked the obligatory questions about my medical history with anorexia nervosa and focused too long on the numbers associated with illness and recovery. It had been years since my last relapse and I was grateful to be in a place of recovery where such focus on numbers and weights no longer triggered me. As she turned the page, I knew things would get interesting.

"Are you sexually active?" she asked.

"Yes," I said, preparing myself for what was to come.

"But it says here you aren't interested in birth control? Are you OK getting pregnant?"

"I assure you, there is no risk of that."

"But..."

Here we go. Maybe one day they'll put "lesbian" as an option on the forms. "I'm gay. I don't have sex with men, so no, I don't need birth control to prevent pregnancy. Call it 'male abstinence.'"

"But what if you have sex with a man?"

"As a lesbian, I date only women."

"Yes, but what if you accidentally have sex with a man?"

"Then it wouldn't be an accident, it would be a crime. And birth control will not undo the risks of sexual violence."

"OK," she said with the same tone as the last doctor. "We'll discuss this more at your next visit." *Sure, because I'll somehow decide to be straight over the next year.* "Whatever." *Don't worry, I won't be back.* It was tiresome trying to find competent medical professionals in Nashville who understood working with a lesbian-identified woman in recovery from an eating disorder. It was rare enough to find someone who understood eating disorder recovery, but I grew tired of the microaggressions involved with yearly preventive exams.

One of the reasons I pursued a masters in social work was to improve client care for LGBTQ+ individuals seeking treatment for eating disorders and other body-image disturbances. I focused my studies at the intersection of eating disorders, trauma, addiction, and the LGBTQ+ community, including marginalized sexual orientations and gender identities. As a cisgender person, I became aware of the privileges I experienced in my recovery journey while remaining acutely aware of the microaggressions and incompetencies I faced as a lesbian-identified client. I was saddened at the lack of information available to students and practitioners about working with LGBTQ+ people with eating disorders, especially those who are transgender or gender expansive. With years of experience now behind me as a clinician, and a partnership with Heidi that has created extraordinary opportunities to speak about the intersection of gender identity and body image, it is my hope to contribute to the literature that can help future clients who engage in the clinical world.

We have had the opportunity to share our experiences with gender-expansive clients who have eating disorders at a number of conferences and events. We are humbled by the depth of experiences shared with us by other providers and trans-identified individuals who frequently speak with us after the presentation concludes. Occasionally, we receive the invitation to remain in contact with these individuals as they engage in similar work or have interest in contributing to this project.

MYLES'S STORY

Note from Heidi and Kayti: We initially met Myles Marcotte at an LGBT conference in California. While the conference was informative, there was an overrepresentation of LGB identities and very few T identities. One disconcerting concern was the lack of all-gender restrooms. How could this be a safe space for people who identify as trans or nonbinary? We brought attention to this during our talk on trauma, subsequently cementing a friendship with Myles. He has generously agreed to share his perspective as a resilient trans male whom we will also be able to call a colleague—Myles is entering the field of social work.

The first therapist I saw for my eating disorder told me that she had never lost a patient to anorexia or suicide. I looked her in the eye with both defiance and despondency and told her, "Well, get ready, because I'm going to be your first." At that point, my eating disorder had become a full-blown effort to make my body and myself disappear completely, and I was dangerously close to actualizing those goals. I entered that eating disorder treatment program at the age of 13, but it would be another year before I returned to my childhood questions about my own gender identity and another five years before my trans identity became something I could share outside my circle of friends.

I would be shocked to find that my therapist when I was 13 had even an inkling that I might be queer or trans, or that my eating disorder and body image issues might be related to my gender identity. Today, as a social worker engaging with youth, I think about this often. When I first began to intern at a middle school, I wanted to create a safe space for LGBTQ youth, but I wasn't sure whether the need was there. We hadn't identified any LGBTQ kids, and they weren't speaking up to ask for that space. However, from the very first time we offered an LGBTQ lunch club, the room was packed with 25 kids every week. This experience has reminded me how crucial it is that mental health care providers don't wait until they know they have a queer or trans client to create a welcoming and adequate environment. Any client we work with could be queer, transgender, gender expansive, or questioning. If we fail to create an explicitly safe environment for them, we miss the opportunity to address the deeper issues of shame, identity, and discrimination that can be tied to eating disorders and other mental health issues.

My hope is that this book can serve as a jumping-off point for providers who want a deeper understanding of the relationship between transgender people and eating disorders. Probably the most widely recognized motivation behind eating disorders in trans clients is the desire to lose or gain weight to be able to suppress or obscure certain secondary sex characteristics. This is certainly a contributing factor for many trans and gender-expansive people with eating disorders. That said, if there were one thing I would like you to take from this book, it is this: Just as no single narrative can cover the diverse experiences of transgender people, there is no single narrative that can explain the variety of ways that trans identity and experience interact with eating disorder development and treatment.

As a social worker, a trans eating disorder survivor, and a community activist, I've had conversations with dozens upon dozens of trans people struggling with disordered eating and body image issues. Every story is unique, which is what makes the case examples used in this book so valuable. My own eating disorder has connected to my trans experience in several different ways. As a young girl, I tried my best to starve myself into the image of the ideal woman so that I might find acceptance and love. At the time, my behaviors were not so directly connected to suppressing secondary sex characteristics as tied to coping with trauma and sexual abuse. Today, as an adult man, I find that I have to out myself as transgender in treatment groups if I want to be honest about the roots of my anorexia. Through my teen years, as gender dysphoria slowly began to set in, my eating disorder became a way to deal with an unidentified dissonance with my body. It became a way to feel autonomy and control over my body and was paired with other methods of body modification. In my early 20s, my eating disorder became a way to alter how others perceived my body. I didn't know whether I wanted to pursue a medical transition, but I lived in a constant state of distress from being misgendered. I had learned to see my body as a "male body" for the time being, but the rest of the world had not. I wore Spandex chest binders that flattened everything from my chest down to my hips. On the days I wore a binder, people would compliment me on having lost weight and tell me how much better and more masculine I looked. I would go home and remove my binder, knowing that I was living in a body they saw as more feminine. As the stress of being constantly misgendered grew, so did my eating disorder as a way to relieve that stress. I felt that regardless of how I dressed or behaved, I had no control over when people would use the wrong name and pronoun. Anorexia gave me the illusion of control over one thing in my life.

The intersection of my eating disorder recovery and my trans identity resulted in me postponing my physical transition for nearly a decade after gender dysphoria began to rule my daily life. When I came out as trans to family members and friends, one of the primary concerns that arose was whether my trans identity was simply a pathological extension of my eating disorder and body image issues. I felt the need to insist that I was not going to change my body, as a way to help the people around me understand that I was not simply self-loathing and delusional. What no one considered at the time was that my eating disorder might be an extension of my life experiences as a transgender person and not the other way around.

I was lucky enough to find the Body Positivity movement as an adult and to learn about the Health at Every Size framework. These communities gave me a means to love and accept my body and to unlearn many of the harmful beliefs about health and beauty that I had internalized. I made a commitment to myself that I would do everything in my power to accept my body as it was before making any attempts to change it. I wanted to be sure—and I wanted everyone around me to be sure—that I was not transitioning purely out of a hatred for my body. In many ways, this was a good experience. It prepared me to handle better the realities of transitioning and the truth that hormones and surgeries cannot erase negative body image on their own.

However, that commitment to completely separate my eating disorder from my gender dysphoria proved impossible. The interconnectedness of the two was ever present, and postponing a transition that would ultimately relieve most of my gender dysphoria only allowed my eating disorder more time to worsen and more years to harm my body. It was not until I was in a psychiatric treatment program for being suicidal that I realized I could no longer care whether others saw my transition as an extension of my anorexia and the body dysmorphia of my early teens. If I wanted to survive, I knew I was going to have to risk the fact that others may see my transition as a deluded attempt to fix an internal problem with an external solution. When I shared my decision to transition with close friends, partners, and family, I was met with concern and even anger that I would make changes to my body while still suffering from anorexia and other mental illnesses.

I have kept a strong faith that the people around me will change their perspective eventually if I live my truth and pursue my own happiness. I am grateful to work today in a field where I can help other trans people who are struggling to make sense of the relationship between their eating disorders and their gender identity or experience. I am also grateful for the chance to contribute to a book that may lead to more competent providers in the field of eating disorder treatment. It is a miracle for a trans person to find the strength to ask for help, and I believe that miracle should be treated with care, compassion, humility, and relevant knowledge.

Therapist competence

Now that you know some of our background and the impetus for this book, we invite you to engage in some reflection about your personal and professional background. We hope you will do so throughout this text and use the various activities and vignettes to support your work with clients. Please take a few moments to discuss the importance of competency in working with transgender and gender-expansive clients and those who struggle with eating disorders and disordered eating.

Competence is the combination of knowledge, professional skills, and personal attributes. Some things that enhance competence include: education and training specific to client need or modality; sensitivity to the idea that identities can be intersectional; knowledge of working with disadvantaged groups; development of new training or research in emerging areas; and protecting clients from potential harm.

To begin our focus on clinician competence, please reflect on a few questions:

- What is your current knowledge level about transgender and gender-expansive clients?

- What is your current knowledge level about eating disorders, disordered eating, and body dysmorphia?

- Are you familiar with your licensure body's ethical standards and recommendations for working with clients within marginalized identity groups?

According to the preamble of the National Association of Social Workers (NASW) Code of Ethics, "the primary mission of the social work profession is to enhance human well-being and help meet the basic human needs of all people, with particular attention to the needs and empowerment of people who are vulnerable, oppressed, and living in poverty" (2017). This mission is grounded on six core values: service; social justice; dignity and worth of the person; importance of human relationships; integrity; and competence. Each of these core values is essential to ethical practice with any client. This book will focus on the competencies needed for working with transgender and gender-expansive clients at this time.

The American Psychological Association (APA) Code of Conduct (2016) calls for psychologists to aspire to five key principles: beneficence and nonmaleficence; fidelity and responsibility; integrity; justice; and respect for people's rights and dignity—key to our work with clients. Despite the ethical guidelines, surveys of trans and gender-expansive people suggest that many mental health providers lack the knowledge and skills required to offer trans-affirmative care (American Psychological Association, 2015). To remedy this, the APA drafted its *Guidelines for Psychological Practice With Transgender and Gender Nonconforming People* (2015). It is a wonderful resource to familiarize yourself with.

The *Standards of Care for the Health of Transsexual, Transgender, and Gender-Nonconforming People,* or *SOC* (Coleman *et al.*, 2012), developed and published by the World Professional Association for Transgender Health (WPATH) is another such resource. As with many similar texts, the WPATH standards are meant to be a guide. According to the standards, the tasks of psychotherapy include:

- Exploring gender identity, role, and expression

- Addressing the negative impact of gender dysphoria and stigma on mental health

- Alleviating internalized transphobia

- Enhancing social and peer support

- Improving body image

- Promoting resilience.

While the WPATH *SOC* document has been criticized for recommending mental health evaluations for trans people seeking transition (we will look at this later), its therapy goals are aligned with our work.

Additional considerations in working with gender-expansive clients include:

- Client self-determination

- Body autonomy

- Parental conflict and consent for care

- Competence

- Reducing the "gatekeeper" role of the therapist and working towards an "informed consent" model

- The therapist as educator, advocate and clinician.

An apology in advance: while gender is a social construct, much of the research on body image (and on gender identity development) utilizes a binary framework. In our chapters, we will make first reference of people "assigned male" or "assigned female" to denote that this is a biological given; for ease of language, subsequent references are often to "male," "female," "boys" or "girls." This is not meant to minimize people who identify as nonbinary or genderqueer. It is imperfect, and we hope the language will change for future editions of this book. Another note about language is the use of preferred pronouns with case vignettes. At times language, such as "they/them" pronouns may feel unfamiliar and can be confusing to those accustomed to singular forms, such as "he/him" or "she/her." We are sensitive to clients' preferences, and hope that our intentional use of their preferred pronouns in this book will also help the reader to acclimate to this.

Thank you for your interest in learning more about working with gender-expansive clients. We encourage you to identify ways your current practice meets the needs of your trans and gender-expansive clients and how you might adapt your practice to further serve them. For those who are "expert" at this, perhaps this text will help illuminate many of the best practices you already engage in.

Heidi J. Dalzell, PsyD, CEDS
Kayti Protos, MSW, LCSW

FOR FURTHER EXPLORATION

Activity: My body: Inner and outer selves

This activity is an exercise that we frequently use with our clients. You will need about 30 minutes for this activity.

Take a piece of paper and fold it in half. On the half that is on the outside, describe your outer self. Write some words or phrases or draw images that reflect how others see you. You might choose to use descriptors that reflect your physical self, roles that others may see, or things that are more readily apparent to others.

Now on the inside of the paper, you describe your inner self. Choose words and phrases or draw images that reflect who you are on the inside. This may be reflective of your truer self, and may include thoughts, feelings, dreams, or other things that are not as readily seen.

Processing

While all of our clients have differences between their inner and outer selves, our transgender and gender-expansive clients may find that the inner and outer selves are markedly different. Think about your own depiction. What are the differences between your inner and outer self as you described them? Do you choose to share a lot in life or very little? Does anything about your description show that you are cis/trans, and so on?

Chapter 1

Meet Our Gender-Expansive, Transgender, Nonbinary Clients

Gender-expansive, transgender, and nonbinary clients have a variety of clinical presentations. And yet, those in our clinical practices tend to share some similarities—most notably, difficulties with body image.

This chapter contains five case examples. Throughout this book, we have changed all client names and identifying information, and some of the cases in this chapter are composites of more than one client. As you read through these cases, it may be helpful to note common themes across them.

If terms like gender expansive, transgender, and nonbinary are unfamiliar, feel free to skip ahead to our discussion of language in the next chapter or consult the glossary in Appendix 3. As for the clients you will meet in this chapter, it may be helpful to understand a few terms. *Transmasculine* (and *trans male* and *trans man*) refer to a person who is assigned female at birth but whose gender identity is masculine. Similarly, *transfeminine* (and *trans female* and *trans woman*) refer to a person who is assigned male at birth but whose gender identity is female.

Gender dysphoria refers to distress that some transgender or gender-expansive individuals may experience at some point in their lives as a result of incongruence between their gender identity and birth sex. This may include discomfort with gender role and primary and secondary sex characteristics (American Psychiatric Association, 2013). Gender-expansive clients have many diagnoses, and it is important to note that not all will meet criteria for gender dysphoria.

MEET JARED

Jared is an 18-year-old client. When Jared's mother first contacted us, our initial impression of Jared (then known by a female name) was of a sensitive young woman who had moderate depression and engaged in mild cutting. The initial stages of therapy went as predicted, with Jared beginning on medication and learning some cognitive behavioral therapy/ dialectical behavior therapy techniques. Despite these interventions, the depression did not lessen and actually seemed to be increasing. When we asked Jared if there was anything else that could be contributing to his depression, he expressed some vague feelings of being "different" but he did not elaborate further.

A few months into the therapy, Jared reached out in an email in which he shared some of his struggles. Jared identified as a boy. He felt best when able to express his preferred gender. This was not acceptable in his religious family or his church community, and he lost several friends after coming out to them as trans. His disclosure also resulted in family turmoil and constant fights with his parents. Jared's prior therapist was a religiously affiliated counselor, and she did not support his gender identification.

Jared was hurt by this lack of support. He started questioning himself and went through a time period in which he recanted his gender identification and instead began to identify as gay. His family and friends were no more open to this identity. Jared's Christian therapist told him that he was going through a "phase" that would stop if his heart were more open to Jesus. She also said that he should use his therapy time to discuss "what's causing the depression." Jared's solution was to repress all feelings connected to these inner struggles. His family and friends were relieved that Jared was "cured."

As Jared repressed his thoughts and feelings, however, his body became the battleground. Jared could not stop thinking about his gender. After much struggle, he again came out to himself as transgender. He began to search for ways to keep this a secret, but secrets are hard to carry on one's own. He discovered that cutting helped to distract him from these thoughts, at least on a temporary basis. He also began to feel more hatred towards his naturally petite body, which did not feel masculine enough. Whether consciously or unconsciously, he began to "bulk up" through binge eating. This resulted in a larger body more congruent with his internal identity. Jared's gender dysphoria decreased as his body became larger. While Jared's mother could see he was happier, she was critical of his weight gain. Jared eventually began to purge in order to lose weight.

While he struggled with his mother's comments and his friends' lack of understanding, Jared felt supported in therapy. We began to discuss the idea of social transition. Were there ways that Jared could achieve a more masculine appearance without binging?

Prior to one of our sessions, Jared decided cut his hair. He could not stop smiling during the session. He also began to dress in a more masculine way, and was often seen as a boy in the world. These tasters of what it could be like to transition further were positive.

Jared began to feel more at ease with his physical appearance. Once again, he came out to his family and friends as trans. Jared was acutely aware that his gender identity caused tension in his conservative family, but he was hopeful that they would eventually accept him. Jared's depression subsequently improved and his binging, purging, and self-injury disappeared for a good part of each month.

Then a pattern began to emerge. With the first signs of his monthly menses, Jared would fall into a depression, and purging would again become a nightly occurrence. Jared's more accepting stance toward his body would disappear. Jared's mother was not supportive of medical intervention to stop menses, and Jared eventually began to cut his stomach, which he associated with his menstrual cycle. The self-injury was usually secretive, and he expressed using it to punish his traitorous body.

The optimism Jared initially felt in identifying as transgender began to shift, and Jared entered a period in which he struggled with depression and hopelessness. This was especially true when he was misgendered by others or fought with his mother over haircuts or clothing choices. Jared's mother gave him mixed messages in terms of his gender identification. For example, she would buy him boy's clothing, but would not call him by his preferred name. When he was invited to a friend's 16th birthday party, his mother insisted that Jared dress "appropriately." She bought Jared a skirt. Then Jared was hospitalized for suicidal thoughts.

Following the hospitalization, Jared arrived for his session stating that he had come to the conclusion that he was "100 percent female." Jared had decided that his family could never accept him as a boy.

Jared's mother sprang into action, purchasing feminine clothing. He began to let his hair grow, put on makeup, and dressed in his new clothing. Jared's friends from his church group were elated that he could finally "glorify God in his body."

Jared reacted with happiness at first, until the depression and self-injury returned full force. During one of our final sessions, he broke down, sharing that the pain felt too familiar. He wanted his family and friends to be happy. "But I'm confused," he said. "I see myself in my body, a girl, with breasts, hips and curves. Then I see me as *myself*"—his masculine self.

Jared's subsequent coming out was met with tears and resentment from his family, and with a rejection from several of his closest friends. Sadly, while self-injuring, Jared cut more deeply, requiring stitches. A trip to the emergency department was the impetus for his family to seek a different counselor for Jared, who was not "getting better."

MEET REESE

Reese is a 15-year-old gender-expansive client who struggles with body dysmorphia, gender dysphoria, and major depressive disorder. Reese's preferred pronouns are "they/them," though Reese sometimes tries out "he/him" in certain spaces on days that Reese feels more masculine.

Reese entered counseling for support with their depression, which complicated their ability to perform in online school. For Reese, the act of logging into their account was difficult—the school listed Reese's legal name—as was the dysphoria associated with seeing their dead name (the birth name) and female gender marker each time they attempted a lesson.

While exploring additional aspects of their gender dysphoria, Reese described significant dissatisfaction with their chest and a desire to pursue surgical remedies once old enough to consent. They described their face and body, especially their chest, in a manner that was incongruent with how others saw Reese; while Reese saw themself as morbidly obese with a chubby face, double-chin, and breasts well over DD in size, others saw Reese as someone with average body weight, a heart-shaped face, single chin, and moderate chest before binding. Reese's difficulties with body dysmorphia intertwined with gender dysphoria, creating a unique presentation of repulsion by their physical features and exacerbating Reese's symptoms of depression.

MEET JIM AND SARA

Jim is a 62-year-old man who has had questions about his gender identity for many years. Jim's preferred pronouns are he/him, although he identifies internally as a woman. Jim's external and internal mirrors differ dramatically. Physically, his body is short, powerful and muscular. He sports a thick beard and is quite hirsute. Jim's internal mirror shows a tall, slim woman with long hair and feminine features. He is aware of the differences between what he wishes for and the reality of his physical appearance.

Jim presents as hyper-masculine. He is often angry. He frequently makes sexual comments about women.

Jim grew up in a conservative Jewish family with a stay-at-home mother and traditional gender roles and expectations. Jim also has close relatives who are Orthodox Jewish.

Jim is divorced and has a grown son. He is currently in a committed relationship with Sara, an attractive woman in her late 50s. Jim's gender identity is a source of conflict in the relationship. He prefers to wear female attire at home, including bras and underwear. Sara can be supportive of Jim's choices, but at other times she struggles. Jim also often comments on Sara's body, focusing on her breasts. He tells her he is jealous that she has breasts, and laments the fact that he can never be a "real" woman.

Sara finds these comments disturbing. She has difficulty being open about this with Jim and has become increasingly depressed.

Jim is not out with his son, his ex-wife, or his extended family. He feels that they would never understand or accept him for who he really is, and that Sara is his only support.

Jim does not place a formal label on his identity.

MEET ROB

Rob is a 29-year-old transmasculine client who manages resources for a sizable information technology company. He uses male pronouns (he/him/his) and identifies as transgender but does not identify with the binary system of gender. Rob describes himself as having some masculine characteristics, some feminine characteristics, and some characteristics that are neither male nor female.

In therapy, we created a visual image of this fluidity by using balls of different colors. Rob created a combination of colors that reflected how he perceived his gender on that day, and a different combination of colors that reflected his gender the previous day.

Rob presents as more masculine at work, given the nature of his profession, and finds himself more comfortable leaning into this part of his gender identity in this setting. He feels more feminine in his relationship with his sister, connecting strongly to the notion of being "sisters" and wants her to continue referring him as a sister despite his transition to a masculine name and pronouns. He describes his role around the house as more agender, focusing on tasks that need to get done rather than the gendered nature of various household responsibilities.

Rob struggles with depression and substance use behaviors that predate his coming out as transgender. He describes his abuse of various medications as a way to "check out" from the unease he experiences with his body. He grew up in a religious family that emphasized living in accordance to the Bible and following traditional roles within the family. Rob previously identified as a lesbian and, at the time, struggled to find acceptance within his immediate and extended family. At the beginning of therapy, Rob expressed a profound fear of how his family would respond to his coming out as transgender. This fear exacerbated his depression and substance use. As he navigated the challenges of coming out in the workplace and at home, Rob's symptoms and sense of comfort with his body ebbed and flowed significantly.

MEET CARLA

Carla is a 45-year-old married cisgender woman. Her child, Adam, identifies as nonbinary. Adam uses they/them pronouns. Adam, now 17, first began to understand that they were nonbinary at 16. Carla struggles to understand Adam's gender identity. She tries to respect Adam's gender identification and has become better at not using Adam's dead name and the pronouns Adam was born with. She wants to be an ally to Adam. "I struggle though," she says. "I don't have the appropriate role models. Books, and other parents, tell me that they 'always knew' their child's gender identity did not fit. My husband and I had no clue."

Carla worries about Adam's safety and future, and at times wishes that she could return to a simpler time. Carla feels that Adam's identification has put a strain on her marriage. "My husband is old-fashioned. As much as I try to understand and be sensitive, he does not. I am in the middle," she says.

While Adam seems to be thriving as they connect to others within the LGBTQ+ community, Carla feels isolated and depressed. She has noted an increasing tendency to unwind with several glasses of wine each evening.

FOR FURTHER EXPLORATION

All of the clients in this chapter share struggles with gender identity, or, in Carla's case, adjustment to a family member's identity. They reflect a range of ages, beliefs, and symptoms.

Think over your roster of past and current clients. How many of your clients might describe themselves in a manner similar to Jared, Reese, Jim, or Rob? How might you show a client that you are open and willing to discuss the topic of gender identity in the therapeutic setting?

Of the clients described in this chapter, pick the client you most identify or connect with. What about his/her/their story resonates with you? If this were your client, what would you like to know or further explore? Take a few moments and jot down your reflections.

Chapter 2

Gender Identity: An Overview

Sophie, a 22-year-old pansexual, gender-fluid client struggling with grief after a breakup with their (preferred pronoun) girlfriend, anxiously awaits their first appointment with a new therapist. Sophie's anxiety increases as they complete the intake paperwork and notice the too-familiar binary options for gender on the form. There is no space to denote identity preferences, preferred names, or pronouns. Sophie fidgets nervously with the ends of their scarf and straightens the line of their dress slacks, wondering if they should have worn something more neutral today.

"Good afternoon, ma'am," says a friendly middle-aged man holding a clipboard. "Nice to meet you. Please, come this way."

"Nice to meet you," Sophie offers, feeling shut down at being automatically gendered yet again.

This is the third therapist Sophie has tried since deciding they needed help.

"How can I help you today?" the therapist asks as he points to a couch for Sophie to sit.

"I'm struggling with some things, but before I go into that, I need to know a bit more about you. Do you have experience working with LGBTQ clients?"

"LGPB....what?"

"Lesbian, gay, bisexual, transgender and queer clients"

"Oh, I can never remember those letters. Too complicated. Yes, I have worked with a number of clients like that. Are you a lesbian?"

"It's not...never mind," starts Sophie, reconsidering their decision to try to correct him. It's exhausting to teach doctors, therapists, and other providers about identity. If this person doesn't understand what the letters mean, how would he understand gender fluidity? Sophie decides to keep things simple and get through the hour as quickly as possible. They will not be coming back.

Sophie's story is a compilation of experiences our clients have had prior to entering our care. Our clients bring many experiences: barriers to accessing treatment; discrimination; trauma; and therapists who are only minimally familiar with eating disorders. This can leave clients feeling misunderstood by the very helpers from whom they are seeking support.

One way to help clients feel more comfortable is through our use of language. Language communicates understanding, acceptance, and knowledge. For example, in introducing ourselves to our clients, we include our own preferred pronouns and identities in this introduction. Our intake forms allow clients to specify gender identity using the term or terms they prefer. Our forms provide a space to indicate their name (as opposed to only their legal name). What may seem like small things to some speak volumes to others.

Sophie and most of the clients in Chapter 1 are *gender expansive*— their gender identities (internal sense of gender) are wider than those of cisgender people (people whose inner sense of gender matches their biological sex). Sophie identifies as both gender fluid (her internal gender identity) and pansexual (her sexual orientation).

In presentations, we introduce people to terminology needed to work effectively within the LGBTQ+ community. This acronym as lesbian, gay, bisexual, transgender, queer, and "plus" represents the more than 45 other identities on this continuum (Bornstein, 2013). The "+" includes the identities of those who are gender fluid, gender nonbinary, pansexual, asexual, and many others.

For some of you who are already fluent with the language, this will be a review. For others, this may be new and slightly overwhelming. That's OK. To help, you will see client examples throughout our discussion of these terms.

Sex, gender, and the body

Imagine a television or movie scene in which a pregnant woman goes into labor. Family members and medical staff surround her. The woman pushes one last time and her baby arrives. The doctor or midwife says "Congratulations! You have a beautiful baby boy." This script illustrates the many concepts that inform our understanding of gender.

In that moment, the child was assigned a label of "boy" based on genitalia. This represents "sex assigned at birth." *Sex* refers to the biological factors of our assigned label and is based on observable body characteristics, hormones, and chromosomes. People who are given a male label at birth are called "assigned male at birth" (often shortened to "assigned male" or "AMAB") and those who are given a female label at birth are called "assigned female at birth" (often shortened to "assigned female" or "AFAB").

Gender, however, is a different construct. Gender involves a social understanding of what the body conveys—male, female, or another gender description. Let's consider the role of the body in gender.

Assignment of a sex (male/female) is also the first gender assignment the child receives (Bornstein, 2013). This body-based attribution lays the groundwork, and as the person's physical body develops and changes, it continues to influence our understanding of gender. As children get older, they develop secondary sex characteristics, such as larger breasts or facial hair, and their bodies assume a shape we think of as "masculine" or "feminine."

Society also "genders" bodies through its expectations about how the ideal male or female body should look or act. People whose bodies look "male" are expected to be muscular and lean; those who appear "female" are idealized as curvy but thin and attractive. People whose physical characteristics are associated with the labels "male" or "female" are expected to behave, dress, and even have personalities congruent with societal expectations of their genders. A "male" should be unemotional; a "female" has more freedom to be emotional.

The body is also a primary medium through which gender identity struggles are played out. For example, transgender males or females may feel uncomfortable in their gendered body or describe a sense of "wrongness." Drew, a trans client, thought the breasts and curves he developed as a teen were disgusting and did not match his *internal* sense of gender, which was masculine. Drew ultimately decided to have surgery to remove his breasts, and hormones provided a way to make his body more congruent.

Other people find that gender-binary labels—male or female—do not accurately describe their *internal* sense of gender. *Gender expansive,* the term used frequently in this book, denotes identity or behavior that is broader than the commonly held definitions of gender. Some labels that fall under the gender-expansive umbrella include genderqueer or pangender, gender fluid, agender, and bigender.

Gender, then, is multifaceted and is much broader than sex or gender assignment. Gender has several major components, including gender identity, gender expression, gender attribution, and gender role (Bornstein, 2013).

Gender identity

Gender identity is "one's innermost concept of self as male, female, a blend of both, or neither—how individuals perceive themselves and what they call themselves" (Human Rights Campaign, n.d.). A person's gender identity can be the same as or different from their assigned sex.

To help with understanding this idea, please take a moment to look in a mirror. If you can, choose a mirror that shows your full body. Scanning your body, what physical characteristics do you notice? What do they say about your identity as male or female? This mirror is your *external* mirror.

Now look at your *internal* mirror—how you imagine yourself in your mind's eye. Again, note what physical characteristics you see. What do these say about your identity as male or female, both or neither? Does what you see in your internal mirror match the external mirror? Does what you see in your internal mirror differ from characteristics typically associated with your birth sex?

Cis and trans identities

As many of us look in these external and internal mirrors, our body and sense of self are congruent. You see a biologically male or female body and self-identify as a man or women. This gender identity is called *cisgender*. The term cisgender has its origin in the Latin prefix *cis,* meaning "on this side of."

For many people, gender identity can be more complex. For example, a client may look in a mirror and see physical characteristics typically thought of as "male," but the client's internal identity is "female"—body and gender identities that are not congruent. This is the definition of someone who would identify as transgender.

George, an older client, describes this, "I look in the external mirror and see an older man. My beard needs to be shaved, my hips are narrow, and I could stand to gain a few pounds. I know what others see," he says. "But in my mind, I am a woman—still slim, but with breasts, long hair, and clean shaven. It depresses me to think that I can never look like that. I've tried putting on wigs and feminine clothes, but I just look like my mother. And who wants that?"

Testa, Coolhart, and Peta (2015, p.10) say that gender identity "isn't what's between your legs, it's what's between your ears." We could not have described this any better.

The complexity of gender identities

Now let's broaden the idea of being *gender expansive* (also called *gender diverse*). You will see these phrases used interchangeably throughout this book. The term *gender variant*, which you may see in other resources, implies a deviation from "normal."

These terms refer to gender identities that differ from cisgender identities. They are umbrella terms that include transgender identities, as well as other binary and nonbinary identities. The related term *gender nonconforming* describes the person's gender identity, role, or expression as different from expectations based on their sex assigned at birth for a given culture (Coleman *et al.*, 2012).

One of our clients, Matthew (he/him), is an example of a person with a gender-expansive identity that is called *gender fluid*. Matthew, an affluent pharmaceutical salesperson, presents to business colleagues in a male body, typically wearing trousers, dress shirts, and other signifiers of "maleness." In the competitive world of sales, Matthew feels very masculine. At home or when caring for his son, Matthew feels more feminine and dresses in a feminine manner. Matthew's gender identity is expansive and fluid, but it is a binary identity (male/female).

Some cultures (e.g., Zuni or Samoan cultures) are more accepting of gender diversity than traditional Western cultures. The term *two-spirit* is used by indigenous North Americans to describe people in their communities who fulfill a traditional third-gender ceremonial role in their cultures. In indigenous cultures, two-spirit people are considered to have both a male and female spirit within them. This term is appropriate only for people of indigenous descent because of the sacred place two-spirit people hold in indigenous culture (Brayboy, 2017).

Nonbinary identities

Nonbinary gender identities include any identity that does not fall within the strict categories of male or female. *Binarism* is the assumption that gender experience is binary and the devaluation of nonbinary experiences of gender. People with nonbinary identities are at higher risk of depression, anxiety, and other mental health concerns (James *et al.*, 2016). While transgender is easily relatable as a binary identity, nonbinary identities can be more difficult to understand.

Jonathan identifies as *agender*—having no gender. Jonathan says "I don't generally attach how I see myself to a gender." Jonathan prefers the pronoun "they" and chooses a neutral presentation to express gender to others. Other terms for agender are *gender neutral*, *genderfree*, or *nongendered*.

Similarly people who are *genderqueer* feel that their primary sense of gender does not conform to the gender binary, or that they are neither "male" nor "female" but somewhere in between or outside these terms. Reese, whom you met briefly in the previous chapter, identifies as genderqueer. Reese describes their (preferred pronoun) gender identity as something outside the "typical" gender experience and does not wish to be gendered as male or female. Reese struggles with their body, which Reese believes "labels" them. Reese hopes to undergo a double mastectomy to remove the physical association between having breasts and being a woman.

Gender expression

People communicate their gender in many ways. *Gender expression* involves how people present gender to the world. Gender expression includes a person's appearance (such as clothing or hairstyles), mannerisms, and other personal traits. Gender expression can shift throughout someone's life, sometimes throughout the day, as people navigate different situations.

Gender expression is important for many reasons. It provides a kind of shorthand that others use to decode gender. For example, a person who has long hair, wears makeup and painted fingernails, and has a curvy body is typically labeled a "woman." This is known as a *feminine* gender expression. Conversely, when we see a person with short or spiky hair without makeup and who has noticeable facial hair, we think "man." This is known as a *masculine* gender expression. Gender expression and gender identity are not always congruent. For example, a person may have a feminine gender identity but because of life situations may have a male gender expression. You may recall that

Jim, from Chapter 1, feels more feminine, but continues to retain a masculine gender expression due to fears about acceptance.

One of the first things that often happens when people become aware that their gender identity does not match their birth sex is a change in outward expression. This is part of the process of social transition. Jared, for example, adopted a new style of dress when he came out as trans, wearing men's jeans, a binder, and oxford shirts. He also cut his hair and wore it in a shorter, spiky style.

A more *androgynous* expression can be seen when someone has both feminine and masculine traits. Sometimes this term is used to denote a person whose gender is difficult to determine visually. Many of you may remember that the late rock icon David Bowie was famous for his androgynous expression. One of our assigned male clients who is very tall and thin does not label identity. They present in an androgynous way and practice moving like a model from *Vogue* to complement this look.

Other gender expressions

There are other expressions of gender that do not fall into these categories.

Cross-dressing involves wearing clothing usually associated with another gender. People who cross-dress may not feel that they identify as the other gender. Reasons for cross-dressing include theatre (drag king or queen), disguise, or experimentation. Cross-dressing has been popularized on American TV, on the show *RuPaul's Drag Race.* Cross-dressing is *not* always associated with sexual fetish, although this is a common misconception.

Gender expression is not necessarily a stable trait. How a person expresses gender will likely change over time and be based on the situation. For example, take a moment to think about what you look like right now. What are your clothing and hairstyle choices? How do these choices differ from when you were a teenager or college student? Have your gender-expression choices changed?

Gender attribution

This phenomenon occurs when we meet someone for the first time and attribute a gender to that person on the basis of an intricate system of culturally specific cues, such as physical appearance and mannerisms (Bornstein, 2013). While it is normal to make assumptions about a person's gender, it's helpful to allow that person the opportunity to self-identify. This includes asking a client about preferred pronouns rather than assuming gender preferences based on appearance.

Gender roles and expectations

The final component of gender is the *gender role*. Gender roles are social constructs—that is, society defines what roles, behaviors, activities, and attributes are acceptable for men and for women. Thus, each culture has its own expectations and guidelines for what people of a given gender "should" do with their lives and bodies.

Take a moment to think about what culture dictates about being a man. What comes to mind? Perhaps you thought about such expectations as being the breadwinner or not demonstrating emotions. What does culture dictate about being a woman? Perhaps you thought about expectations such as being a mother or dressing in a way that is sexy. How do you fit within these role expectations? Have these expectations remained stable, or have they changed for you?

Gender expectations are reflected in how a person displays emotions, chooses a career, engages with others, nourishes the body, and interacts with families.

After they begin the internal or external process of transitioning, many of our transgender and gender-diverse clients find it difficult to decondition themselves from the gender role expectations placed on them based on their assigned sex. This internal conflict may explain why they may voraciously embrace their inner gender identity—sometimes even with an exaggerated sense of masculinity or femininity.

Tara, a 23-year-old transgender woman, describes her awareness of gender expectations. Tara was raised in a household with strict gender roles and expectations. As a female, she now feels pressure to wear tight-fitting clothes, to make feminine food choices (such as choosing a salad), and to participate in pilates and more traditionally feminine exercise programs.

Sexual orientation and gender identity

Most cisgender, transgender, or gender-diverse humans have romantic and/or sexual attractions to others. *Sexual orientation*—our enduring emotional, romantic, sexual, affectional, and relational attractions to other people—should not be confused with gender identity.

Sexual orientation is determined by one's personally significant sexual or romantic attractions and by the way in which someone self-identifies. Sexual orientation is rarely black and white. A person may be emotionally and romantically attracted to women but sexually attracted to men—or may be romantically attracted to men but sexually attracted to neither men nor women, to use two examples. The possibilities are vast.

One of the common areas of confusion among parents and professionals who are newer to the field concerns the intersection between gender identity and sexual orientation. The general rule of thumb here is to remember that gender identity (not assigned sex) guides how we label sexual orientation. A trans woman who is sexually attracted to a man, for instance, is straight; a trans woman who is sexually attracted to a woman is lesbian. Some of our trans clients choose to identify their sexual orientation as *queer* to represent a path that is different from cisgender heterosexuals. Each person defines their own sexual orientation and uses the language they provide when referencing their identities.

Cisgender body privilege

What does having privilege mean to you? How does this connect with what you have just read about trans individuals and about body image?

Privilege is the inherent benefits that certain groups of people have by being part of a majority group. Some examples of privilege are white privilege, male privilege, and heterosexual privilege. Another example of privilege is cisgender privilege. Cisgender privilege refers to benefits gained as a result of the congruence between assigned sex and gender identity. Many of these privileges are body based, as you will see in the list below.

Cisgender body image privilege checklist

1. My body matches my gender identity.

2. I can expect others to "gender" me appropriately (he/she) when they see/interact with me.

3. My appearance does not cause strangers to ask what my "real name" is or question my pronoun choices.

4. People do not stare at me or at my dress.

5. If I present myself to family as my true gender, I do not have to fear rejection.

6. I can use the restroom of my choice without being scared that others will ask questions, berate me, or ask if I am in the wrong place.

7. I do not have to diet excessively or binge to achieve a body congruent with my identity.

8. Bodies like mine are represented in television, movies, and other forms of art.

9. My validity as a human is not based on how much surgery I've had.

10. Strangers don't assume they can ask me what my genitals look like and how I have sex.

11. If I enter a residential setting, such as a college dorm or a treatment center, I will be housed with others of my gender identity without being asked about my body parts or whether I have fully transitioned.

12. People don't tell me that I look like a "real" man or woman.

13. People do not use incorrect pronouns for me or persist in doing so, even after they have been corrected.

14. If I need hormones because of an inability to produce them on my own, it will be considered an "obvious" need and my health insurance will likely cover the expense.

15. When initiating sex, I don't have to worry that they won't be able to deal with my body.

16. I can find clothing and shoe sizes that fit me.

17. People do not do a double take when my voice does not match my gender expression.

18. The gender and the name listed on my official forms of identification match my gender presentation and the name I use.

19. When I walk into a clothing store, I will not be harassed for shopping in the men's or women's section.

20. People I do not know well do not ask me personal questions about my body, my history, and my identity.

FOR FURTHER EXPLORATION

The below activity was originally referenced in Rob's experience in Chapter 1. Enjoy.

Activity: Understanding my gender

This activity is a tactile way to understand a person's gender understanding. Our office contains a bin of many differently colored balls. The client then identifies a color to represent "male-ness," a color for "female-ness" and a color for each aspect of their gender, using any language the client has for these other genders. Some choose a color to represent "agender" while others are unsure of the language but know that there are more than two genders/colors involved.

If you do not have a bin of colorful balls, please take a moment to create something that can represent the balls. A simple suggestion is to find a set of highlighters or markers with at least four or five colors and a few sheets of paper. On the paper, use the different colors to create "balls" by drawing and filling in circles. Cut out the circles and you will have a two-dimensional version of the basket of colorful balls.

Take a moment to reflect on your understanding of your gender identity at this time. Remember that "male-ness" and "female-ness" do not have to balance one another but can stand on their own spectrums. Are there other genders represented? Is there space for no gender or agender?

Assign a color to each aspect of gender identity that comes to you. Perhaps green represents "male-ness." How many green balls are in your gender identity pile, or how masculine do you know yourself to be? Perhaps blue represents "female-ness." How many blue balls are in your gender identity pile, or how feminine do you know yourself to be? Perhaps orange represents "agender" or "nongendered-ness." How many orange balls are in your gender identity pile, or how agendered do you know yourself to be? Continue for as many aspects of gender that resonate within you.

Take a look at your gender identity pile. What colors are most represented? Are there colors in this pile that surprise you? Are there colors or quantities of colors that would be different if you completed this exercise at a different time period in your life?

Chapter 3

Body Image: An Overview

A brief activity sets the stage for our discussion of body image.

Begin by writing the words "My Body" in the center of a piece of paper. Spend the next five minutes associating with these words. Notice what thoughts/words come immediately to mind and what come later.

After five minutes, look at your word associations. How many of these words are objective? Subjective? Evaluative? Positive? Negative? Gendered (male, female, neutral, fluid)? Do any show internal dissonance? Do any of the words point to privilege or lack thereof?

As clinicians, it is helpful for us to look at our sense of our own bodies. When doing this exercise, there are a range of responses. Most clinicians have a mix of words, some objective, some evaluative. It's also interesting to see how many of the words on these lists are gendered in nature. For example, "pretty" or "beautiful" are words typically associated with females; "handsome" or "hunky" with men. "Slender" or "graceful" may be considered more female, while "ripped" may be more male. Some words, such as "strong" and "capable," are more gender-neutral.

Ours is a gendered society with distinct categories of "male" and "female." These divisions are less biological than one may initially think. Newborn children are classified as male or female based on their genitalia. While the body may be the initial source of this distinction, "male or female" is also a social construct (Lorber & Moore, 2011). The language above is one example.

Body image, loosely defined, is how people see themselves when they look in the mirror or when they picture themselves in their minds. We'll give a fuller definition in a moment.

In people who are gender expansive, body image is influenced by biological factors (body size, shape, parts) that communicate maleness or femaleness (both social constructs) to others.

In Chapter 1, you met Jared, and in this chapter you will meet Cayden—two clients who have struggled with eating disorders and body image. While not all clients who are gender expansive grapple with body image, many do. Jared and Cayden had body-image concerns before they recognized and embraced their identities as transgender men. Both struggled with biological aspects of their bodies, such as the monthly menstrual cycle. Jared also experienced rejection by friends in his church youth group for not meeting their expectations of what a "girl" should look like or how a girl should behave.

Defining body image

Thomas Cash, a pioneer and one of the pre-eminent experts in the field of body image, defines body image as "the multifaceted psychological experience of embodiment, especially but not exclusively one's physical appearance" (Cash, 2011). He states that body image encompasses one's body-related self-perceptions and self-attitudes, including thoughts, beliefs, feelings, and behaviors—those things unique to identity.

Body image is the picture we have in our minds of the size, shape, and form of our bodies and our thoughts and feelings concerning these characteristics and body parts at any given moment. While this definition is somewhat long, several parts of it are important. The definition highlights the visual and imaginal nature of body image, the attitudinal and evaluative aspects of it, and its changeability, which can occur on a moment-to-moment basis.

Dr. Ann Kearney-Cooke, an expert in the treatment of eating disorders, first shared this definition at a training program. There are six key components of body image: *cognitive*, the thoughts and beliefs about bodies; *perceptual*, referring primarily to body size prediction; *affective*, the feelings about one's body; *evaluative*, the judgments about one's body; *social*, the acute awareness of others' feelings, attitudes, and beliefs about bodies; and *kinesthetic*, or the sensed fluidity of movement.

Body dissatisfaction is the difference between an individual's actual body and the person's ideal body size or shape. Jared, a naturally more petite youth, often discussed such body dissatisfaction, and used binging as a way to achieve a stockier, more masculine body. Like Jared, many of our transgender clients struggle with feelings of discontent about their bodies.

An important distinction concerns the difference between body dissatisfaction and body image distortion. When people think of disordered eating, they often envision the classic image of the very thin woman looking into a mirror and seeing an obese person. Body image distortion is a state in which people's perceptions of their own bodies are inaccurate in some way. For example, clients who are diagnosed with anorexia often see certain body parts as being much larger than they actually are (body size misperception). There is some evidence that children with obesity also misperceive size, underestimating their weight (Sarafrazi *et al.*, 2014). Body-image distortion can lead to unhealthy food and exercise behaviors. Body-image distortion is often coupled with perfectionism, a focus on symmetry and gendered norms of male/female body ideals. While Jared was dissatisfied with his then-female body, his perception of its size and appearance was quite accurate.

For gender-diverse clients, body dissatisfaction is not an unhealthy phenomena, although body-image distortion often is. Clients should not be forced to live with the feeling of being in an incongruent body when their internal sense of identity diverges so greatly, or to accept body functions like menstruation or beard growth. That said, many of the other more traditional interventions connected to body image— most importantly, loving self-care—are key.

A colleague of ours, Dr. Stacy Hunt, looks at body dissatisfaction in transgender clients as similar to the unhappiness seen in people who experience certain medical conditions and interventions. They may elect to have reparative surgery to resolve their body dissatisfaction. For example, would a young man with unresolving gynecomastia (a condition in which there is an increase of male breast tissue) be told that he should "just live with" the situation? Would we deny someone who has had a mastectomy breast reconstruction? Yet transgender clients are often forced to fight for medical interventions.

Body image develops throughout the life cycle, most notably in late childhood and adolescence. Body-image difficulties can affect people of all ages. Studies have shown that body-image concerns can arise in young adulthood, midlife (McLean, Paxton & Wertheim, 2010), and in older adults (Baker & Gringart, 2009). While negative body image seems to affect females more often than males, body dissatisfaction is seen in all genders.

Influences on body image

Cayden is a 24-year-old graduate student in college. He will be having top surgery to enable him to have a more masculine looking chest within the next few weeks. Cayden initially sought counseling as a teen struggling with anorexia and self-harm. At that time, Cayden's gender expression was feminine, although Cayden was "a tomboy" and enjoyed sports. While Cayden's father welcomed the tomboy, his mother frowned on this. Cayden also attended a high school that valued physical appearance as a means of attaining popularity and esteem. Cayden's sister was striking and very popular. Cayden was more shy and had difficulty making friends. Cayden's mother and father often commented on his sister's appearance, and Cayden struggled with these comparisons. Cayden's shorter stature and curvier body type became a source of distress and hatred.

Cayden's story illustrates many of the aspects of body image presented in this section. In focusing on Cayden's body image in the early stages, we will briefly illustrate how influences at the time interacted with gender identity formation. In practice, it can be challenging to ferret out all of the influences on one's own body image, analogous to putting together a 500-piece jigsaw puzzle. While Cayden's initial presentation had some foreshadowing of what he later described as living in the "wrong body," Cayden's first years in therapy were spent treating the anorexia and self-harm, which we viewed as a response to familial and peer pressures. When he determined that he was transgender, it was like placing the final piece in the puzzle.

Many clinicians believe that body-image concerns arise only within the context of eating issues and are based on a drive for thinness. One of the most often cited theories is called the Tripartite Influence Model of Body Image (Thompson *et al.*, 1999). This model proposes three formative influences on body image: peer, parents, and the media (sociocultural factors). Peers, parents, and the media provide messages about the ideal body and about societal acceptability. The Tripartite Influence Model further suggests that body-image and eating problems arise through two processes: internalization of the thin ideal and appearance comparisons. This is certainly the case for some clients. While interpersonal, familial, and cultural factors are important, they are only a piece of the puzzle.

Researchers have attempted to apply the Tripartite Model across clinical populations and have found evidence that it applies well to young white heterosexual women. There was less support for other groups, including for women of color (Awad *et al.*, 2015),[1] or for women who identify as lesbian or bisexual (Huxley, Halliwell, & Clarke, 2015). While sexual orientation and gender identity are different, this example shows that the Tripartite Model is not as robust as it may appear. The Tripartite Model also has mixed feasibility in men (Klimek *et al.*, 2018). This model has not been assessed in gender nonbinary clients.

Gender-expansive and transgender clients seem to have different pathways to body-image disturbance. What makes it complex is that, like Jared and Cayden, many initially present in bodies associated with their assigned gender. They may not actually recognize or disclose their actual gender identification until later. Parents can influence body image, sending messages about acceptability. Media can also influence body image (there are very few transgender role models in the media). While the "thin ideal" is sometimes the perceived motivator, in trans clients body image tends to be more layered. For example, while some of our clients who develop restrictive eating are seeking a thinner self, they may not be using the eating disorder to look like a runway model. Instead, they may be using food restriction as a way to make the body smaller and more female or to suppress secondary sex characteristics.

Another model of body-image development is Cash's (2011) cognitive behavioral model. According to Cash, all cultures transmit ideas about which physical standards are valued or devalued, and these ideals are disseminated through mainstream and social media. He also stresses the importance of gender-based expectations (masculinity/femininity) in these messages about ideal bodies.

Cash points to the role of interpersonal experiences (peers, parental and familial messages, and modeling) on body image. For example, children who are considered "cuter" get more attention from caregivers. Cayden often felt this with his sister. Peer comparisons also play a role, and teasing can be especially detrimental.

Research is finding that transgender people who can "pass" better (likely because they demonstrate attractiveness norms) may be more accepted by others (Bockting *et al.*, 2013). Some examples of passing

---

1   Much of the current research does not include diverse voices. For more information on cultural aspects of body image, we suggest referring to Awad *et al.* (2015), Anderson-Fye (2011), Franko & Roehrig (2011), and Schooler & Lowry (2011).

are Carmen Carrera (actress and model) and Aydian Dowling (trans activist and fitness enthusiast). Carmen and Aydian are beloved role models among our clients. They also have bodies that are attractive, toned, and buff—body ideals that may not be attainable for many transgender people.

Certain personality factors also heighten vulnerability to negative body image (Cash, 2011). These include perfectionism, low self-esteem, and insecurity or self-consciousness. Cayden had all of these characteristics prior to embracing his trans identity. His self-esteem and confidence have improved.

Gendered influences on body image

What does it mean to have a male body? A female body? These are questions our clients ask themselves before and after social or medical transition. Standards attached to the male and female bodies underpin body-image attitudes—the organizing constructs or schemas about body image and attractiveness. How can we include nonbinary bodies in this conversation?

In the female body, a heteronormative, thin ideal applies. To be attractive, women must be pleasing to "the male gaze" (Murnen, 2011). Characteristics of the ideal female body: thin, yet curvy in "the right places," large breasts, rounded derrière. Women are also socialized to dress in ways that are attractive to men, such as wearing tight clothing and high heels; to use makeup, and to shave their legs. Telling a woman that she looks too "boyish" or "manly" is usually an insult.

Cayden struggled with these ideals prior to transition. Cayden was not naturally tall or thin, and preferred not to wear makeup. Cayden liked comfortable, sporty clothing. This did not fit the preferences of Cayden's family or Cayden's image-conscious high school.

Western male body ideals, however, are more mesomorphic, characterized by visible—although not overly large—musculature coupled with low body fat (Tylka & Sabik, 2010; Lavender, Brown, & Murray, 2017). Men and boys are socialized for a V-shaped body: broad muscular shoulders, tight abdominal muscles, a narrower waist. While leanness is a factor for men, it is based around a drive for muscularity.

Murnen (2011) points out that the emphasis for women's bodies is on how they *look* while the emphasis for men's bodies is on how they *act*. Additionally, while powerful women are often expected to appear a certain way, power for men does not necessarily involve physical perfection. People born into the assigned gender of male may feel less pressured about their appearance, which is not as highly equated with masculinity. Trans men, who have been socialized with a female mindset, may more highly subscribe to the idea that in order to be a "real" man they have to be muscular and buff. Similarly, Jim, from Chapter 1, struggled with not having the physical attributes he most associated with being female.

Developing positive/negative body image

Children and teens are exposed to many body-based messages that relay acceptance, pride, or lack thereof. These messages form the basis of body-image schemas. Schemas involve enduring beliefs, experiences, and generalizations about body and self. For example, a child who is picked last for sports may believe, "I'm not athletic" or "I'm too fat." A child who receives excessive attention about physical appearance may believe, "My value resides in how I look" or "I am pretty."

People who develop more negative body schemas often use negative coping mechanisms in order to manage these schemas. Examples include reassurance seeking, appearance-checking, or eating disorders.

Cayden received many messages about attractiveness and femininity. While Cayden never felt particularly good, puberty tipped the balance into body-image distress. He gained weight and began to develop secondary sex characteristics, including widening hips and breasts. The predominant schema, however, was "something is not right with my body." With no frame of reference that said to Cayden, "I am transgender," he interpreted this as "what's not right is that my hips, breasts, and so on make me look fat." Cayden went to war with his body, attempting to restrict food to diet away curves. We initially believed that the function of Cayden's eating disorder was increased peer and familial acceptance. It was only after multiple hospitalizations that we began to suspect that for Cayden, the body would never be "right." Eventually, Cayden recognized his authentic gender identity and began his transition.

Body image disturbances/clinical concerns

How is body image linked to clinical concerns? People with body-image disturbance can present in a number of ways. These include the following:

- *Gender dysphoria.* Gender dysphoria involves a deep discomfort between a person's physical or assigned gender and the gender with which he/she/they identify. Much of this discomfort involves *body dysphoria*—the sense of being in the "wrong" body or being seen as the wrong gender (Saleem & Rizvi, 2017). While gender dysphoria may become evident during puberty, it can begin as early as age four or five. Gender dysphoria can cause significant distress and can co-occur with the other clinical concerns.

- *Social difficulties.* Body-image concerns (as well as identifying as gender nonconforming) often lead to social difficulties, including social anxiety. Tantleff-Dunn & Linder (2011) call social interactions the "looking glass" through which our experiences with others reflect back messages about ourselves. Disorders related to body image, such as eating disorders, are often characterized by greater social anxiety and self-consciousness. Cayden, for example, often struggled with social anxiety. With nonclinical samples, Davinson & McCabe (2005) found that among adolescent girls, more positive body image predicted more positive relationships with both genders. For boys, more positive body image predicted more positive relationships with girls.

- *Sexuality issues.* Body image also affects sexuality and sexual self-concept (Donaghue, 2009). Body-image dissatisfaction hampers sexual behavior and expressiveness and inhibits the quality of sexual experiences. Cash, Maikkula, & Yamamiya (2004) found that sexual performance is related to stronger sexual self-concept, less anxiety and fewer worries about body image. This was true for both males and females in their study.

- *Anorexia nervosa* is characterized by restrictive eating patterns; weight loss (or lack of appropriate weight gain in children); difficulties maintaining a suitable body weight for height, age, and stature; and often a distorted body image. People on the gender-expansive spectrum may eat restrictively for a number of reasons. These include control, an increased sense of their own identity and self-esteem, distracting from painful feelings, or to reduce the appearance of certain body parts.

- *Bulimia nervosa* is characterized by a cycle of binging and compensatory behaviors such as self-induced vomiting, laxative or diuretic use, or compulsive exercise, designed to undo or compensate for the effects of binge eating. People with bulimia have excessive concern about body shape and weight. People on the gender-expansive spectrum may engage in binge/purge behaviors as a way to discharge anger, to cleanse or purify the self (especially when there is also trauma), or to release tension.

- *Binge eating disorder* is characterized by eating large quantities of food (often quickly and to the point of physical discomfort); feeling a loss of control during the binge; experiencing shame, distress or guilt afterwards; and not regularly using compensatory measures to counter the binging. Behaviorally, people with binge eating disorder may demonstrate concern with body weight and shape, although they may be of average weight. People on the gender-expansive spectrum may binge eat as a way to comfort or numb, to distract from painful feelings, or to make the body larger.

- *Other specified feeding and eating disorders*. This category is a "catch-all" classification for those who do not meet strict diagnostic criteria for anorexia, bulimia, or binge eating disorder but still have a significant eating disorder. This specification includes people who eat restrictively but are in a larger body or who purge in the absence of binge eating.

FOR FURTHER EXPLORATION

- What have been your greatest influences on body image? Family, friends, other important experiences? Select the top two and explore these further in writing or collage.

- What are your most enduring body schemas? How do these affect you as a person and a therapist?

Chapter 4

Developmental Perspectives on Gender Identity and Body Image

"I've always felt like who I see when I look in the mirror is not 100 percent me," begins Robbie, age 16. "My gender journey[1] has been one of recognizing that 'tomboy' is not who I am, although that was how I used to identify. I was born into a female body, but it didn't fit."

This articulate teen has had many unique experiences during his (now the preferred pronoun) gender journey. Born to supportive parents, Robbie has been exploring his gender. Robbie is a talkative teen, born with significant physical disabilities, but these have not slowed him down. Some of Robbie's early memories of nonconformity included hanging out with the boys, a love of all sports, a dislike of dresses or feminine clothing, and an aversion to the hypersexual Bratz dolls ("I despised them"). He often felt like "one of the boys." During his monthly period, "I got very depressed by the reminder that I was female," he says. Robbie felt as if he lived between genders.

Robbie credits the TV show *I am Jazz* for helping to affirm his trans identity. "It was like a light went on," he says "Tomboy, no, boy, yes." Next in Robbie's gender journey: gender-affirming hormones. His parents are fully supportive of this step.

A developmental perspective

We see clients of all ages and at all stages in their journeys. It is helpful to adopt a developmental lens in thinking about them. Shaffer and

---

1   Like all the terms we use in this text, the term gender journey, while commonly used in the field, does not appeal to all. We ask clients their preferences—and sometimes use alternative terms like gender exploration or gender story.

Kipp (2013, p.2) define development as "systematic continuities and changes in the individual that occur between conception and death." Development encompasses two important processes: maturation (a biological process) and learning (a psychological process based on experience).

This chapter will explore how gender identity develops, with a special focus on the intersection between gender and body image. Using a developmental perspective, we will proceed chronologically by age and developmental stage, highlighting key areas of development in terms of gender and body image.

Assumptions of this chapter

Prior to looking at gender identity development, let's pause to describe several assumptions of this chapter:

1. All children are born into a body that contains primary sex characteristics (body structures directly concerned with reproduction), hormones, and a brain.[2] These characteristics are connected to their assigned sex.

2. Children are exposed to information about gender (gender norms) and body ideals. These messages come from parents, peers, the media, and culture at large. Thus, gender roles, and what it means to be a gendered person in our society, are socially constructed ideas. Our current generation of youth is working hard to change these set ideas about gender.

3. Gendered messages are powerful. While they significantly influence cisgender kids and adults, they can be damaging to people whose identities are incongruent with the gender binary or for those whose inner sense of self differs from their assigned sex.

4. This lack of congruence can cause sadness, confusion, or the need to hide. The "true self" may even go underground, and the person may create and present a false self.

---

2   Some theories of gender identity development look at the role of biological influences, genetic/epigenetic or hormonal and neural mechanisms, and brain anatomy differences in the etiology of gendered behavior and gender nonconformity. For an example, please see McCarthy, Auger, & Bale, 2009.

5. As clinicians, our role is to help clients navigate their unique gender stories, without an end goal in mind (e.g., embrace or reject trans identity); the journey *is* the goal.

Infancy and childhood

Gender identity development begins prior to birth, with the parents. When couples find out that they are pregnant, they often wish for a boy or girl. In the United States, a newer trend is for couples to have a "gender reveal," in which they announce the coming baby's sex at a party. At birth, it is still common for doctors to announce "It's a boy!" or "It's a girl!"

Along with imagining the baby's sex, parents may also imagine what the child will look like physically. These fantasies often involve idealized gendered norms, such as a female "Gerber baby" with symmetrical features, curly blond hair, and a pink bow. At this point in the development, it's generally acceptable for the baby to be chubby.

Infancy and early childhood are a time of tremendous growth across all areas of development. There is the biological legacy (hormones, chromosomes, body parts, brain) of natal sex or assigned sex that is "male" or "female." The assigned sex sets the stage for parents and family members, who are the first people to communicate gender expectations. Human beings, then, are active constructors of cognitive schemas, including gender, in continuous interaction with the environment (Martin & Ruble, 2010).

During infancy, the child grows and matures rapidly, mastering important life skills. These physical changes are accompanied by rapid changes in the child's cognitive and language development. Lawrence Kohlberg, one of the first developmentalists to offer a theory of gender identity development, describes an increasingly complex understanding of gender, beginning with the recognition of basic gender identity, progressing to gender stability, and concluding with gender constancy (Kohlberg, 1966, 1969).

At about the age of two years, children begin to develop a sense of "me," recognizing themselves in mirrors and in photographs (Smolak, 2011). This lays the groundwork for noticing differences among people. Children become aware of the physical differences between boys and girls. Even before the of age three or four, most children can label themselves as a boy or a girl, according to Kohlberg's (1966) stage of *basic gender identity*. In this stage, children know that they are assigned male or a female, but do not understand that gender is a constant, at least in terms of biological assignment.

This is also the first developmental stage in which children begin to make comparisons to each other. The labels "boy" or "girl" are based on physical characteristics that children observe in themselves and others. Zosuls and colleagues (2009) note that the use of gender labels occur at approximately 19 months of age. These labels generally conform to gender norms, such as awareness that boys have short hair or dress in pants, or that girls have long hair, wear bows, and like to play with dolls. By age four, most children understand that assigned sex does not change—Kohlberg labels this stage *gender stability*. For many people who are gender expansive, the internal sense of gender does develop and change, particularly during adolescence. Additionally, biology can be medically changed to increase congruence between internal gender identity and the body.

Sandra Bem's Gender Schema Theory (1981) provides additional insight into how people become gendered within our society. Gender schemas are gender-related beliefs that influence behavior. For example, children make distinctions between "things that boys do" and "things that girls do." Children express gender preference through a number of media, including clothing, hairstyle, preferred names or nicknames, more masculine or feminine body language, chosen friends, and relationships. Their social behavior may be aggressive, dominant, passive, or gentle. It is within these preferences and in their relationships that there may be a foreshadowing of gender nonconformance, such is the case with Robbie's story.

All pre-pubertal children engage in play involving gender expression and roles. It is not unusual for both cisgender and transgender children to try to various roles of boy or girl. Toys seem to be one of the primary sources of gender differentiation as such schemas develop. Gender-diverse children and preteens often have an interest in toys and activities we may associate with their nonassigned gender. Robbie, for instance, loved Pokémon trading cards. Family members often discourage such preferences, informing children what is acceptable gender-wise. In addition to stereotypical interests, children learn more about the gendered nature of subtle patterns of behavior. For example, an assigned female may be told that aggression is not "ladylike." An understanding of these gender norms occurs as early as age four-and-a-half to five (Giles & Heyman, 2005).

What, then, of gender-nonconforming children? According to Grossman and D'Augelli (2006), gender-creative children (the preferred term) may begin to label themselves as the nonassigned sex or may express nonconforming preferences as early as age six, with a mean age of 10.4. Gender-creative children may or may not maintain these preferences throughout life, and puberty blockers are often used to allow them more time to transition socially and fully establish the longevity of these preferences.

One rule of thumb for decisions on medical transition is the "insistent, consistent, persistent" guideline. Are children firm in expressing cross-gender preference? Do they do so consistently? Are they steadfast in this preference? Transgender children may engage in cross-gender expression or role-playing. They may state that they wish they are in the other gender's body or ask for body parts that are associated with their preferred gender. A child with a more gender-fluid presentation may express feeling agender or nonbinary, or may refuse to ascribe to typical masculine or feminine assignments (Janicka & Forcier, 2016).

Many (but not all) of our other clients recall early examples of feeling "different." Some may not experience distress about bodies until confronted with expectations of gender from peers. When Cayden (assigned female) was six, he attended a swim party at a friend's house. All the girls were dressed in bikinis. While Cayden also wore a bikini, he felt extremely uncomfortable and wished that he were wearing swim trunks. This was the genesis of a long struggle with body hatred. Many clients describe being shamed for expressing gender preferences incongruent with their assigned sex. This may cause them to "go underground" (Janicka & Forcier, 2016), suppressing feelings about cross-gender preferences and refraining from cross-gender activities. Thoughts, feelings, and behaviors may become more secretive. These thoughts and feelings, however, still exist.

KAITLYN AND KYLE'S GENDER JOURNEYS (GENDER CREATIVITY)

Kaitlyn and Kyle (assigned male) are six-year-old twins. Their father and his husband are both gender-sensitive clinicians who do their best to allow them to explore gender as they wish. Kaitlyn is a shy child who enjoys quiet activities like drawing and playing with dolls. Kyle is a character. His hair is long, pink is his favorite color, and he loves "interpretive dance" performances, complete with tutu and tiara. When asked if he is a boy or girl, Kyle most frequently responds "girl," but will sometimes answer "boy."

In earlier versions of our diagnostic manuals, we may have pathologized a child such as Kyle, terming nonconformity or variance as disordered. The newer diagnostic label, gender dysphoria, carries far less stigma. The diagnosis of gender dysphoria in childhood is made when a child feels an incongruence between the experienced (psychological) gender and the sex assigned at birth (American Psychiatric Association, 2013). The diagnostic criteria focus on observable factors, including preferred dress, gender roles, or toys. The criteria also include a dislike of one's physical anatomy or the desire for the primary and/or secondary sex characteristics that match one's experienced gender. Children must experience significant distress to be diagnosed with gender dysphoria. This distress is often focused on a desire to change the body, or persistent discomfort with certain body parts, most often genitals.

Body-image development also becomes more complex as the child gets older. Children assigned both male and female receive messages about acceptable bodies for children and adults. Many of these messages concern disapproval of peers who are seen as "fat." Children as young as preschool may express such disapproval, as well as weight bias (Harrison, Rowlinson, & Hill, 2016; Pont et al., 2017; Zuba & Warschburger, 2018). Body-image concerns and dieting have been seen in assigned females at age five or six. There is also evidence of gendered differences among preschoolers, with young boys expressing the goal of muscularity and girls the goal of thinness (Smolak, 2011).

Children under the age of 13 can develop eating disorders. The incidence is about three in every 100,000 children, according to a study published in the *British Journal of Psychiatry* (Nicholls, Lynn, & Viner, 2011). Early-onset eating disorders tend to involve food restriction (anorexia, avoidant restrictive, or unspecified). There are many causal factors, such as the possible role of strep infection, temperament or personality profile, family history and functioning, and stress (Poppe et al., 2015). The latter category is quite broad, and it is difficult to segregate identity-related stress. As of the writing of this book, there have not been studies looking at eating disturbances in younger gender-expansive clients.

As clients move toward adolescence, gender and body-image pressures become more intense, perhaps because of the development of secondary sex characteristics and the onset of puberty.

Adolescence

Adolescence begins between the ages of about 11 and 14. Early adolescents are capable of more advanced cognition and understand the long-term consequences of their actions. Socially, they are more independent from parents and more reliant on peers. Physical growth is rapid, and sensory development does not always keep pace with these physical changes.

One of the most important changes in adolescence is puberty. Puberty is the process of physical changes as one's body matures and becomes capable of sexual reproduction. Hormonal changes during puberty result in the development of secondary sex characteristics. For both males and females, this includes changes in stature and the development of underarm and pubic hair. Girls begin to menstruate, their hips widen, and their breasts develop. Boys become more muscular, their testicles enlarge, and they sprout facial hair. This, of course, is the brief version of a complex series of processes.

Puberty is a challenging time for transgender youth, who may experience significant gender dysphoria. The development of secondary sex characteristics and the onset of menstruation solidifies undesired physical development. A repeated theme for many of our clients assigned female at birth is significant dysphoria that corresponds with the monthly menstural cycle. Dutch studies suggest that puberty-blocking drugs may be appropriate for trans children, giving them more time to explore and consolidate gender preferences. Research on young adults following puberty suppression (de Vries *et al.*, 2014) shows that this has great promise in promoting positive outcomes. Psychological functioning is better, with decreased incidence of gender/body dysphoria, mood disorders, and behavioral problems. Children treated with puberty blockers also seem better adjusted socially and demonstrate a sense of well-being. This may be in part due to children "passing" more easily as their preferred gender (de Vries *et al.*, 2014).

During middle adolescence, ages 15 and 16, there is a continued movement toward independence and a focus on identity development. This stage also heralds an increase in sexuality, with a focus on dating relationships. A trend has been short-term serial monogamy, where teens move from one relationship to another, trying out various partners. This may also be a time in which teens explore same-sex attractions.

One of the most important psychological processes of middle adolescence is identity development. Erik Erikson (1968) presented the most well-known theory of adolescent identity development. Erikson describes identity as a fundamental organizing principle that develops throughout the lifespan. Identity provides a sense of sameness—as well differentness—to others. It is this uniqueness that allows people to function autonomously from others. Positive peer relationships support esteem and identity development (Nawaz, 2011). For gender-diverse adolescents, relationships with peers who are also exploring gender can be very important.

During early and middle adolescence, social comparisons become more pronounced. We often see this play out in terms of body comparisons. Several researchers have looked at the connection between social comparisons and negative body image, and they have found that peers are quite influential. Overweight girls, for example, are frequently teased about appearance, which was a predictor of body dissatisfaction, eating disturbances, and low self-esteem (Thompson et al., 2007). Similarly, Healthwatch, a UK group, conducted a focus group with LGBTQ youth, many of whom attributed body concerns to pressures to conform, experiences of bullying, and social comparisons (Healthwatch Northamptonshire, 2016).

Following puberty, the core self, including transgender identification, is stable. According to Pleak (2009), following pubertal changes, transgender identities are unlikely to change. In other words, being transgender is a variation and not a phase.

Body image continues to develop. Adolescent boys respond to the changes of puberty, especially those involving the development of secondary sex characteristics. There is some evidence that pubertal timing (early puberty, more age-normed puberty, or late maturation) may affect body image. Those who are late bloomers are more at risk of negative body image (Ricciardelli & McCabe, 2011). These studies did not differentiate cisgender and gender-expansive teens.

During middle adolescence, an even greater number of girls express preferences about thinness. Wertheim and Paxton (2011) found that at preadolescence, 40–50 percent of girls express a desire to be thinner; by adolescence, this proportion increases to 70 percent. Body dissatisfaction is most prevalent when an individual's body characteristics do not conform to cultural beauty ideals. This becomes important when you consider that many of our transgender or nonbinary clients reject beauty norms, putting them at higher risk of body-image concerns. Changes brought on by puberty, such as menstruation, may also be difficult, resulting in the feeling that they no longer have control over their body.

During middle adolescence, many of our clients may experience a drop in self-esteem because of body dissatisfaction. In our trans and gender-expansive clients, the most prevalent thing we see is a dislike of specific body parts—commonly breasts, hips, abdomen, the waist, or legs. They may express that these body parts identify them as "male" or "female" and feel "alien" or "not right." This dissatisfaction can lead to increased dieting with the goal of de-emphasizing certain body parts and promoting a more androgynous appearance. There may also be overeating, with the goal of appearing bigger (and sometimes more masculine), or as a means of self-punishment.

Middle adolescents who experience gender dysphoria may also self-injure due to body hatred. We all remember the changes our bodies went through during puberty. This can be overwhelming. Girls suddenly receive attention from boys and men as their bodies become curvier and more feminine. Trans girls are at a disadvantage as their bodies are less curvy and traditionally feminine. At this age, boys compare themselves with others who are more or less physically developed. For trans boys, these comparisons often result in negative self-attributions as their bodies are less muscular and broad than other boys. These developmental changes, then, are challenging for clients along the gender-expansive spectrum.

Jared, whom we met in a prior chapter, would often self-injure with the goal of punishing hated body parts. The most frequent targets were his breasts, thighs and hips, which Jared thought labeled him as female. Larry, a 14-year-old transgender client, would self-injure to experience a sense of control over his body as he felt powerless over the changes associated with puberty. His cutting became a way to cope with living in the "wrong body."

Bullying may play a role in self-injury and in other difficulties that gender-diverse youths encounter. In a large survey of sixth to tenth graders in 2009 (Kosciw *et al.*, 2010), the National Institute of Child Health and Human Development found that 37 percent had been a victim of verbal harassment and 32 percent had been subjected to rumor spreading. Bullying is often centered on the teen's physical self, and our gender-expansive adolescents are extraordinarily vulnerable to bullying. Teens experience bullying in a very intense and personal way, and it can shake self-esteem tremendously. Gender-nonconforming behavior has been consistently associated with an increased likelihood of experiencing bullying and harassment in peer groups (McGuire *et al.*, 2010). While it may seem contradictory, some teens, like Larry, see self-harm as way to gain a sense of control or to ground themselves.

Eating disorders often begin during this time and can be related to these developmental changes. The mean age of onset for anorexia is 16–17. It is slightly later in bulimia, with a mean onset of 18–19 years. As with Cayden, adolescents may present with eating disorders or self-harming behavior before they (or we) recognize the connections to gender identity.

At this stage, adolescents often try on different identities. While some gender-expansive adolescents express certainty about their gender, clearly articulating the vision of self as their preferred gender 10, 20, or more years into the future, others are less certain. For adolescents who are more certain, middle to late adolescence may be a time to at least begin exploring the use of hormones. While in no way a "magic bullet" for body dysphoria, initiating hormones can sometimes quiet body-image concerns as teens begin to see the first signs of changes.

Many teens come out during adolescence. Some adolescents have concerns about coming out, while others feel comfortable coming out to family and peers. Supportive environments are invaluable, as are associations with the LGBTQ+ community. Coming out can involve choosing a preferred name, and changes in dress and presentation. These changes can have positive effects on body image.

Late adolescence/emerging adulthood

Additional development occurs during emerging adulthood between the ages of 18 and 22. Late adolescents have a firmer sense of identity and greater emotional stability. They are more future oriented and self-directed. Cognitive abilities are also more complex.

In the time leading up to late adolescence, the typical weight gain for those who are assigned female is four to nine pounds, which may be difficult. Most assigned females have reached full physical maturity by the age of 17 (although it may take others until the age of 19 or so to reach full maturity). Assigned males generally reach the final stages of puberty by this time. They may continue to grow taller and to gain weight and muscle mass into their 20s.

Late adolescents often pull away from family, yet the adolescent still needs family support. While transgender adolescents may fear peer or family rejection, there is also a strong desire to be seen as the core self.

Relationships continue to mature and there is more freedom. Many youths move away from home or enter college. These young adults may previously have delayed dating—often because of a reduced availability of potential partners—and college provides a larger pool of dating partners. Bungener and colleagues (2017) found that transgender adolescents had fewer sexual experiences than same-age peers; approximately half of their sample reported "falling in love" and experimenting with some form of sexual intimacy. These differences could in part be linked to body image, as sexuality and sexual confidence are inherently linked to body confidence and positivity (Pujols, Meston, & Seal, 2010).

The increased freedom afforded young adults may also allow those who have not previously been able to come out to live more openly. It is important to help gender-expansive young adults to select college environments that will be validating and supportive. Too many times, this is not the case. Stolzenberg and Hughes (2017) studied transgender students as they entered college. These students reported their emotional health (especially with regard to mood) to be below average, experiences of bullying and pressures to conform to gender norms. They also struggled with a lack of trans-affirmative housing, and managing differences between their preferred and legal names. Trans students were more likely than peers to seek support from counselors and through peer and social networks. There was also a significant sense of agency among transgender students, with a high number participating in social and political activism.

Young adults often have their first independent medical appointments at this time, allowing them to make decisions about gender transition. Many of our clients prefer to begin the process of medical affirmation/transition prior to college, if they have not already done so. This may also be a time when young adults begin the process of changing their names or gender markers in preparation for being identified this way in college.

Adulthood

JIM'S GENDER STORY

Jim, discussed in Chapter 1, has had a gender story similar to that of many of the adult clients we work with. At age 62, he is actively exploring gender with the help of his partner, Sara. Jim describes "always feeling different." While he yearns to look and dress like a woman, he jokes, "I feel like a woman. But if I dressed like a woman, I'd look like my grandmother. And she was not pretty."

Prior to dating Sara, Jim was married for many years. He has an adult son. Jim has gone to great lengths to conceal his longing to be female, choosing a male-centered job and demonstrating his macho in social exchanges and a love of football. His quieter, more academically inclined son is often embarrassed by Jim's aggressive masculinity.

Jim began cross-dressing after he divorced. He met Sara a couple years later. Initially she was comfortable with his cross-dressing as long as he did it only at home. After an argument concerning wearing female undergarments to work, Jim consulted with a counselor. She encouraged him to wear female clothing. "She wanted me to create the persona of Jeanette," he says. "It scared me and Sara. I thought she might leave." Jim left this counselor, seeking a gentler approach. While it is imperfect, Jim is trying to find a balance that the couple can live with.

For various reasons, many adults like Jim revisit gender later in life. Some describe knowing about a cross-gender identification and "living in costume" for many years. Not all adults choose to openly affirm their identity, often due to fears of rejection. Jim did not believe that his ultra-religious family would be able to accept any differences in gender identity. Jim chose the path of living authentically at home, and in his relationship with Sara, but not in the wider community.

Other adults do choose to fully embrace their gender identity at older ages. Doreen, a 56-year-old trans woman has been on hormones for a year-and-a-half and is scheduled for top surgery. She is finding the transition challenging, especially in her workplace. It's often helpful to investigate corporate policies and climate prior to transition.

As in other developmental stages, adult clients continue to be subject to stressors. The Minority Stress Model (Meyer, 1995) suggests that transgender people face stigma and prejudice beyond general stress faced by cisgender people. Examples of minority stress include rejection and discrimination, violence, difficulty accessing trans-affirmative services, internalized transphobia, expectation of rejection, and the need to conceal identity (Bockting *et al.*, 2016). The degree of distress rises if the client has multiple marginalized identities, such as being a transperson of color or belonging to a religious group that does not support being transgender. These situations often result in psychological distress. Other clients demonstrate remarkable resilience.

There may also be barriers associated with physical intimacy and starting a family. Transgender people can identify as any sexual orientation. While not all clients do, some trans-identified people experience sexual arousal disorders, low sexual desire, and anorgasmia (Klein & Gorzalka, 2009). Sexual problems may be hormonal or may be a result of body-image concerns.

Studies (e.g., Pujols *et al.*, 2010) point to the connection between positive or negative body image and sexual satisfaction. This study operationalized body image as body-part satisfaction (e.g., satisfaction with stomach or breasts), concern with body size, and comfort with one's body in front of a partner. As with prior studies, negative body image was associated with sexual avoidance, whereas positive body image was associated with higher frequency of sexual intimacy, adventurousness, and satisfaction. For transgender adults, then, it would be important to select a validating partner and to fully communicate concerns about body image.

For adult clients, family support continues to be key. Family support can be a protective factor in coping with minority stress. Family rejection, however, can be high, as can violence within the family (Grant *et al.*, 2011).

FOR FURTHER EXPLORATION

- Think about your own gender journey. What were the most important influences (early memories) on your own gender-identity development? How did you look or act like a boy or girl? How would it feel to be a nonbinary gender (androgynous or two-spirit)?

- Have there ever been times when you have related to the idea of the false gender self? If so, what were these times?

- Be a media critic. Grab a handful of magazines (especially those read by teens) and tear out advertisements. What messages do these ads convey about body ideals? Did you find examples of androgynous bodies? How many bodies do not conform to body ideals? How do you feel within your body and self when viewing these magazines?

Chapter 5

Gender-Based Coming-Out Process

"To be more free."
"To let my body catch up to my brain."
"To have people look and see *me*."

These statements, shared with the permission of our clients at varying stages of the coming-out process, describe their hopes and dreams as they progress to a place where they feel more fully authentic and can disclose a gender identity that differs from their birth sex. In some cases, this journey will involve an internal acceptance of gender identity. Other people who disclose their gender identity go on to transition socially and physically to be able to live as their true selves.

Coming out is the process of understanding, accepting, and valuing one's own gender identity. This can be an important part of each person's gender story. While gender identity is internal, external disclosure of this identification may allow people to feel more at peace internally, to seek others who identify in similar ways, or to begin the process of social transition (expressing gender identity through clothing, preferred name, preferred pronouns) or medical transition (hormones or gender-confirmation surgeries, such as top surgery). Many of our clients choose medical transition because the external body communicates gender to the outer world, and medical transition can be transformative. Thus, as people come out to themselves and others, they often choose to disclose their identities by altering their physical appearance so that it matches their internal sense of self. A person involved in the coming-out process may also become more open within existing social communities or become part of communities that are more affirming.

This chapter will provide an overview of the coming-out process. We will look at how the coming-out process can affect body image. We will include case vignettes highlighting the pros and cons of coming out based on client experiences.

The uniqueness of each person's process

Everyone's coming-out journey is unique. It is shaped by their comfort level, the safety of their environment, and how ready that person is to share in an intimate way. It is important for clinicians to meet clients where they are, to help clients pace when needed, to fully explore the pros and cons of disclosure, and to develop a plan. One of the clinicians whom we supervise recently had a client in her mid-20s whose coming-out plan evolved from complete secrecy about her trans identity to telling *everyone* in her life simultaneously. Fortunately, the clinician felt that it was important for her client to explore whether slowing down could be beneficial. In this case, the client's internal coming out (to self) felt so good that she thought it would feel even better to tell others. When the client explored the pros and cons of coming out so widely and quickly, she became aware that she had not fully thought through the process. The clinician helped this client to identify the safest people to come out to (in this case, her mother) and role-played how she would do so. Eventually, this client chose to come out to all the key people in her personal life and took more time to investigate her employer's work policies. The process was therapeutic and validating, and the client was met with support from her family, friends and, ultimately, her employer.

Creating safe, therapeutic space for coming out

Safety is an important aspect in coming out. Safety is the ability to show one's deepest self without fear. This is not as simple as it may appear. Think about the things that you choose to show to others and those that you hide. Perhaps you've hidden a love of a certain type of music from friends or others who would laugh at this preference. Perhaps you have hidden something deeper, such as a religious or spiritual belief. In this case, there may be many reasons for doing so: maybe you are still exploring or questioning this belief and don't feel fully comfortable embracing it. Maybe you live or work in a community where this belief could jeopardize your job security or even your safety. For example, many of our Muslim neighbors stopped wearing their headscarves in the aftermath of the September 11 terrorist attacks. While there are a number of reasons people hide important aspects of self, most involve safety.

Our clients will struggle with coming out (sometimes even to one's self) if we cannot create safe space. Educate yourself on issues related to gender identity, ask about and use preferred names and pronouns, and do not push clients into taking steps they are not ready for. While it's OK to guide or ask, "How do you think your mother would react if you share what you are thinking about your gender identity?", it's not OK to tell a client, "You should try dressing as a boy" or "You must tell your family at this point." Although these points may seem evident, we have heard too many stories of therapists who give this type of advice.

One of our clients, for example, related that his former therapist told him he must bring a change of clothing and change in her restroom prior to sessions. On one occasion when he chose not to present as "Sadie," she insisted that they spent the entire session processing his "resistance." He did not return to therapy for many years. When he did, he was able to voice a genderqueer, rather than trans identity, which provided much relief to him and his partner. Similarly, we hear stories of therapists who do not use preferred names and who do not support medical transition even in the face of severe dysphoria, and other examples of invalidation.

Models of coming out

With those initial thoughts in mind, let's look more closely at the coming-out process. Gender identity is a person's internal sense of being male, female, neither of these, both, or other gender(s). All people form a sense of internal gender identity as a part of human development.

The process of gender-identity formation occurs within interpersonal relationships and is culturally influenced. People who are cisgender experience the messages they receive from family, friends, and culture as congruent to who they are as males and females. People who are gender expansive, however, experience these messages dissonantly. Thus they may be told, based on their assigned sex, that their body should look a certain way. These messages may also be connected to dress, actions, or even to feelings. Many of our clients experience a sense that the messages they have received are "not right."

Clients may not immediately connect this sense of "not rightness" as being related to their gender. Clients may initially believe that the internal dissonance relates to sexual orientation, only to realize later that they are actually straight. For some people, this may mean multiple coming-out experiences, each of which may carry a unique set of challenges for the client. Another example of multiple coming-out experiences may involve clients who initially identify and come out as gender fluid but then discover that their identity is transgender—and then come out again as transgender.

For example, Jared, whom you met in the introduction, initially believed that he was gay, which he disclosed to family and friends. After intensive therapy for body image and disordered eating, Jared at first identified as gender fluid, then realized that he was actually transgender (and straight). He disclosed to family and friends that he was trans, but was met with such a visceral lack of support that he retracted it. After a psychiatric hospitalization, Jared's family decided to discontinue therapy, so we do not know what subsequently occurred.

Transgender models of gender development look at the adaptive processes through which clients manage this inner sense of self and identity.

While coming out is not a new term, models of coming out as gender expansive or transgender have not yet caught up with our current understanding of gender as nonbinary and fluid. For example, Arlene Lev (2004), one of the most influential writers on the gender-based coming-out process, describes gender as a wholly binary process:

> Gender identity is considered core identity, a fundamental sense of belonging to one sex or the other. The sense of being a "man" or "woman" is an essential attribute of self; many people would have trouble identifying their sense of "self" outside the parameters of "man" or "woman." (p.4)

Gender identity is not necessarily binary, but can include a range of expressions. Family and friends, however, may have more difficulty understanding nonbinary identities, such as gender fluid, gender neutral, and agender.

Lev is currently in the process of updating her model. We find the current one sufficient with some simple adaptations. These adaptations are relatively simple, such as changing Lev's language to reflect a view of gender more expansive than the binary view she described in 2004.

As we describe the stages of coming out, we will share the story of Liam, a 27-year-old transgender client.

Gender Identity Emergence Model

The coming-out process involves a complex interaction between developmental, intrapersonal, and interpersonal processes. Coming out does not occur sequentially or in a linear way for most people. These stages are also not meant as an assessment of the maturity of an individual's gender identity. Gender identity emergence can occur at any age and is influenced by the person's unique psychosocial challenges and assets (Bockting & Coleman, 2007). While coming out is traditionally thought of as a singular process that occurs within the individual, in many cases the therapist and/or family go through a parallel process.

Lev's (2004) model includes: 1) Awareness; 2) Seeking information/Reaching out; 3) Disclosure to significant others; 4) Exploration (Identity and self-labeling); 5) Exploration (Transition issues and possible body modification); 6) Integration (Acceptance and post-transition issues). The stages below are adapted to fit the histories and experiences of our clients.

Awareness/Confusion/In or out

The Awareness stage involves the person's increased cognizance of and understanding that internal gender identity differs from natal gender. In the Awareness stage, the central therapeutic task is to provide a non-judgmental environment in which clients can share their gender stories and feel acceptance and affirmation. Lev (2004) describes the therapist as the "midwife" of the client's story.

A significant factor that often underlies the recognition that a person may be on the gender diverseness continuum is body-mind dissonance—the idea that one's body and identity are not congruent.

Many of our clients relate stories of being aware from an early age that their bodies did not match their self-image. Kimber, who was assigned male, recalled the resentment that she (preferred pronoun) felt when playing dress up. Kimber felt as though her body was meant to wear tutus, rather than the overalls that her mother chose for her.

Some children and adults flirt with gender identity by trying out clothing and behaviors that diverge from cultural expectations—an initial coming out. How this is met by others can form the basis of how and when they come out. For example, Kimber was told that friends would think Kimber was "a sissy"; Kimber's father was harsh and used the word "faggot." Years later, Kimber remembers these words and feels hurt and confused.

Children and adults may hide their authentic selves for fear of censure or abandonment. This was the case with Jim, whom we met in Chapter 1. Jim's traditional family expected him to be "manly": muscular and fit. Further, he was told that he should marry, have children, and be a provider. As a teen, he had come out to himself as trans but could not tolerate the possibility of family rejection. Many people, especially those who are older, choose to acknowledge an expansive gender identity only to themselves. Others hide it even from themselves because of fear of stigma.

There may also be a lack of appropriate role models for those exploring non-cis identities. Thankfully, this seems to be changing with role models such as Caitlyn Jenner and Jazz Jennings, who are in the public eye as openly trans. Both have transitioned socially and medically. Jazz has the distinction of being a role model to our younger clients. Jazz's family is extremely supportive.

Reactions of family and friends can affect willingness to come out. Mikayla, an adorable seven-year-old transgender girl, came from an open and supportive family. She told the family, "Mommy, God made a mistake with me. He put me in a boy's body." Mom, dad and older sister embraced Mikayla fully, and family members have become active allies, supporting not only Mikayla but other young people who are struggling.

Let's turn now to Liam's story.

Liam initially entered treatment because of the dangerous trifecta of bulimia, self-injury, and alcohol abuse. He (preferred pronoun) described feeling "alien" from peers and had a deeply rooted sense of being "bad." As a child, Liam, assigned female, played with the boys and became his father's football buddy. Everybody thought this was cute, and that he was a "daddy's girl." Liam often fantasized that he was a boy, but "knew" that he was a girl. On occasions when he was invited to girls' birthday parties, and had to wear feminine attire, Liam felt very uncomfortable. Later,

Liam attended an appearance-conscious high school. He responded by buying stylish clothing and wearing his hair long and straight. Liam's bulimia started in his freshman year, and self-injury quickly followed. In his sophomore year, Liam started drinking heavily and continued to self-injure. The school required that Liam seek therapy, and though he did, his self-destructive behaviors did not abate.

During Liam's junior year, he came out in therapy, and to his family, as lesbian. He began dating other girls, engaging in a series of short-term relationships. Liam also cut his hair and assumed a more masculine appearance in keeping with Liam's identification as a butch lesbian. Liam's initial coming-out experience was not positive. His mother staunchly disapproved of his dress and sexual orientation. Her own drinking increased. Liam's mother would binge drink and fight with his father about Liam's hair, dress, and behavior. The lack of support triggered a period of heightened self-destructiveness; although Liam had initially felt better in his body, he now felt guilty about how his butch/masculine appearance affected his family. He decided it would be better to be dead and attempted suicide. Following a long hospitalization, Liam's parents agreed that it was better for Liam to dress comfortably rather than to harm or kill himself.

Shortly after the hospitalization, Liam stated, "I don't feel fully female," identified as gender fluid, and later identified as a trans man. The latter realization came during the time of Liam's menstrual cycle. He described a profound sense of "wrongness." He wanted to live in a male body.

During the early stages of Liam recognizing his authentic gender identity, Liam "came out" to himself and his therapist, enabling him to more fully explore his gender story. He did not initially choose to come out as trans to his family, due in large part to his mother's alcohol abuse.

Seeking information/Reaching out

In the Seeking information/Reaching out stage, awareness cedes to action. Gender identity moves from an internal/intrapsychic process to an external/interpersonal process.

In this stage, clients enrich their understanding of gender identity by gathering information. This can mean researching what it means to be gender expansive, using online sources (e.g., Planned Parenthood, Human Rights Campaign), reading biographies of people who are openly out as transgender (such as Ryan Sallans, Jazz Jennings, or

Skylar Kergil), or seeking support from a therapist versed in working with people of a range of gender identities. Similarly, families seek information or support. Lev (2004) defines the therapeutic task of facilitating linkages and encouraging outreach. It helps to be aware of local supports and to provide appropriate referrals.

Increased awareness allows for increased support. Many people choose to join LGBT or transgender support or social groups, which provide a sense of universality and acceptance. Parents may seek out other parents whose children are exploring their gender identity (the Parents, Families and Friends of Lesbians and Gays (PFLAG) group is a wonderful resource), or read stories about families who have had children who are transgender (e.g., *Transitions of the Heart,* (Pepper, 2012)).

Liam devoured several books, learning all he could about what it meant to be trans. Our initial efforts to connect him with a wider social network failed abysmally. He staunchly refused to consider the supports available through his school. His school's LGBT group did not have any trans kids. The kids that did routinely attend were too "weird" and too "out." He was not ready to connect to a group where he would be the only out trans member. Liam needed to take baby steps.

At this time, several other gender-expansive kids with whom we were working also needed peer support, and a therapy group was born. The group's focus on gender and its distance from the school community made Liam feel comfortable. He quickly developed close bonds with several of the group members. Liam's participation allowed him to embrace his identity more fully and to explore the benefits of disclosing his identity to a wider circle. These benefits included being true to himself, easing the burden of secrecy, expanding his circle of support, and beginning medical transition.

The group was also honest about the downside of disclosing trans identities to others. Some group members had experienced transphobia or had been rejected by others within their communities, such as the church or workplace. They had also experienced microaggressions such as misgendering, and safety concerns such aggression and bullying. This provided Liam with a balanced view of coming out to others. Liam reflected on this feedback before progressing with coming out, a growth for this normally impulsive young man.

The deciding factor was the hope that his parents may be able to embrace him as *himself*, rather than as their "problematic daughter." Group members shared stories about similarly unsupportive parents who were able to eventually became allies. Liam began to let go of the responsibility for his mother's alcoholism. He understood that the problem was hers and that it would not be improved were he to remain his female self, and to sacrifice his true self.

Liam's bulimic symptoms and cutting lessened. He began to feel more at peace with himself. At the same time, he again began to experience more dissatisfaction with his gendered body. He knew that family support, especially financial support, would be essential in attaining the male body that he needed.

Disclosure to significant others

Gender emergence is what people traditionally think of as "coming out." During this stage, the person discloses gender identity to significant others: parents, spouses, partners, family members, friends, and other significant relationships. The therapist's role is to help in this disclosure and to facilitate integration of the new identity.

Many of our clients have been shocked at the lack of surprise from supports when they verbally affirm their identity as transgender, genderqueer, and so on. These clients have often been "out" in terms of clothing choices or experimentation with body modifications such as haircuts, breast binding or padding, or genital tucking. One of our clients, a 20-year-old college student, came out while home for Christmas. His parents had seen the photos of his short hair and masculine attire on Facebook. They were not surprised. Body communicates a lot.

Liam initially embraced the identity of butch lesbian and dressed in a way which he felt worked for him. This experimentation helped him to discover the more congruent identity of trans male.

In working therapeutically to assess who to disclose to, what to disclose, and when to disclose to others, *why* is one important factor to explore. Specifically, what does the client hope for in sharing? Is the client seeking acceptance or support? A way to access additional services (e.g., transition)? Changing a form of address, such as asking another to use a preferred pronoun? It can be helpful to ask clients about their expectations of the other person's response, and to share that there can be a variety of responses, ranging from outright acceptance to rejection.

Even for families that have had multiple clues to a client's identity, a confirmatory conversation can be surprising, and families may not be as immediately supportive as one might hope. Some families go on to become much more affirming. The same can be said for friends and social communities.

One helpful technique is to help the client create a visual depiction of their circles of support, a model that has been used in person-centered therapy (see Figure 5.1). The circle includes the important people in a person's life and is a visual depiction of closeness versus distance. Picture a bull's eye. The center of the bull's eye represents the self or person who is considering coming out—"Me."

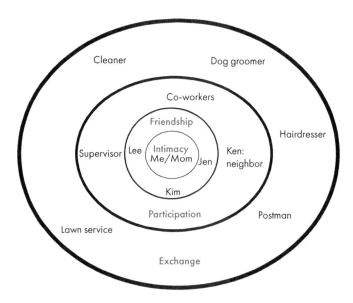

Figure 5.1: Circle of support

Within the "Me" ring is the person's Intimacy Circle—the people who are the closest, most intimate relationships. The Intimacy Circle includes people who are emotionally close. Liam chose not to include his grandfather, who had made transphobic comments, in the circle at all. Some people choose to include people who may provide other types of support in addition to emotional closeness, such as financial supporters. One of our clients included his father in the Intimacy Circle, since he was the only one who could help pay for testosterone.

The next ring, the Friendship Circle, contains the person's friends. Friends can be excellent supports, especially when a person's family of origin is emotionally disconnected.

The Participation Circle includes co-workers, the local community, acquaintances, and other people with whom the person interacts with on a frequent basis but who are not friends.

The Exchange Circle is more transactional. This can include, for instance, a hairdresser, the home cleaner, or business associates.

Some people who create circles of support do not label their circle's rungs. There is really no right or wrong way to do this.

We suggest that the first people to come out to are those who are in the Intimacy Circle. Some things to explore include:

- With whom do you have the closest and most trusting relationships? The safest relationships?

- Have you shared other things with this person that may have been challenging? What do you want to achieve through sharing?

- How do you think they will react?

- How will you feel if their reaction is not as accepting as you may wish?

- Are there body changes and modifications that you are thinking of, and would you like to plant seeds to discuss these further?

- What kind(s) of support will you need for these modifications?

While disclosing to significant others does not necessarily need to be done within a therapy session, this is often helpful (as is role-playing prior to such a session). Within coming-out family sessions, we often draw on our backgrounds as educators to help with the clarity of disclosure. Some important things to discuss with parents or significant others can include:

- What gender identity is—and that it is not necessarily a binary concept

- That "gender identity" is not a phase

- What it means to be trans, genderqueer, and so on. Some terminology, like genderqueer, can be difficult for some people to understand

- That their loved one's mental health may be connected to their ability to work toward greater understanding and support

- That ultimately the person may seek to transition in some way. How and when may need further exploration, and answers may come later.

Finally, smaller disclosures are often better. Except in cases of very severe dysphoria, it is helpful to allow families to adjust first to their family member's core identity and their plans for social transition. After some adjustment time, family members tend to more readily support medical transition. Patience is difficult, but this can make a difference. Sharing with a mom that her beloved daughter is a trans male and is planning on beginning testosterone the following week is not kind, nor is it generally effective. There are no hard-and-fast rules about timing, and some families ask these questions immediately. Of course, this guideline may need adjustment if the slower process causes unbearable distress or overly exacerbates the client's body dysphoria.

While it is ideal coming out to family and friends in person, when people feel comfortable, another alternative is a coming-out letter. There are some wonderful online templates that people can use. Letters have the advantage of being more easily digested by some families who need time to take things in. Letters are also a good way to let extended family know about gender changes.

Liam decided to come out to people in his Intimacy Circle in phases. He began by coming out to some close friends and his brother. His friends were fully supportive and easily adapted to his preferred name and pronouns. Similarly, his brother appeared unsurprised. His low-key reaction ("Awesome, bro") was powerful for Liam, and this first successful foray into disclosing his identity to family paved the way.

Liam was afraid to tell his mom and dad but his desire to begin medical transition trumped his fears. In a family therapy session, Liam shared that he felt "more male than female," and that this was causing many of his struggles.

His parents asked many of the questions that we expected, wondering whether this was another "phase" that Liam was going through. The assurance that he had been exploring this in therapy for some time was helpful. Liam's mother was also concerned about his safety and how others would react. His father was silent and took the information in stride.

Liam's mother's worries turned out to be well founded. Within Liam's school and among his teachers, Liam received mixed responses. His school had no guidelines for accommodating trans students. The school counselors were not versed in working with trans youth. Liam gamely attempted to educate them, but it was often an uphill battle. One counselor, for example, refused to use his preferred name because it was "too hard to remember." Liam was also bullied, being tripped up in the school hallways. School personnel told him that if he "wanted to be a boy he needed to toughen up." Liam ultimately made the decision to seek cyber schooling. This provided space to further explore his gender identity more safely.

Exploration—identity and self-labeling

Lev (2004) terms this stage "Identity and self-labeling." It is a time to explore further what a trans identity means following disclosure to significant others. Here, we slightly adapt Lev's description of this stage, and feel that the therapeutic task during this stage is to support increased articulation and comfort with one's internal identity.

Having a trans or gender-expansive identity is not a one-size-fits-all experience, and for many this exploration and social transition dovetail. There may be experimentation with hair, makeup, binding, or other things that can help to support identity. These changes typically precede medical transition. Clients at this stage may also move into a different identity on the gender spectrum, such as a client who more comfortably embraces a fluid, rather than trans, identity.

Identity exploration and self-labeling is a process. Clients may spend years in this phase of exploration. One of our clients, Kurt, who is in his 50s, has gone through a significant amount of time in this phase. Kurt was assigned male at birth and today identifies as gender fluid. He has experimented with many aspects of transition, including selecting clothing that feels more feminine but is still "men's" clothing, such as pink polo shirts. Kurt takes a small dose of estrogen. Kurt's body image has improved and his marriage is intact. His wife also continues to explore the importance of these choices for her.

At this stage of exploring identity, Liam continued to wear his hair short, to select men's clothing, and to bind and wear a packer. While his family financially supported these choices, they (especially the packer) were a source of conflict. His mother also had difficulty with him being out at his job, and she often did not use his preferred name. Liam felt emotionally isolated from his parents. While he understood that his mom had not yet caught up to where he was, he was vocal—and at times combative— about these microaggressions.

Liam's summer involvement in a trans youth camp meant time away from family, and this provided a respite. Liam's parents compromised with the desire for medical transition by allowing him to start birth control to stop his periods. Liam's family continued therapy while he was away.

Exploration—transition issues/possible body modification

A further stage of exploration involves looking into medical transition and body modification. Here, the clinical task is to provide an open and supportive space to explore. Many clients ultimately recognize that they cannot be content until their physical body matches the one they see internally.

Lev (2004) suggests that therapists help clients resolve transition/ body modification choices and act as advocates. This may mean sharing resources, responding to questions about how other clients have handled transition, or writing letters of support for hormones or surgeries. It is important not to push our own beliefs about what is most helpful. Allow clients to explore and develop their own conclusions about the pros and cons of medical interventions.

As Liam entered adulthood, he decided to seek hormones and top surgery. With each of these body modifications, he has grown more confident and secure.

Integration—acceptance and post transition

People in the Integration phase of coming out further synthesize their identity. The therapeutic task is to support adaptation to transition-related issues (Lev 2004). Clients who have completed some form of medical transition often discuss how good it feels to be in the "right body" but also how strange it feels to integrate into life as their preferred gender. One of our straight trans women in her 20s, for example, did not fully comprehend how difficult it would be to be on the receiving end of male attention. She was ill-prepared for men's advances, and fearful of violence should she attract the "wrong" man (one who was transphobic). We also see other intimacy issues. Jim and Sara, who we met in Chapter 1, had an active sex life prior to his coming out. Subsequently, Sara avoided sexual intimacy. While she still loved Jim, she was not a lesbian. Sara felt as if Jim wanted to *have* her body, rather than just admire it. Fortunately, they have a solid relationship, and are actively working on how to resolve this.

Other issues of concern may include:

- Reactions of religious and community organizations, and acceptance within these circles

- How extended family will respond

- Perceptions by society at large

- For married or partnered people, how children will react. Will they experience prejudice because they have a non-conforming parent?

- Will they will face other stigma? Within healthcare? Within employment?

This is hardly an exhaustive list, but it provides some starting points.

Coming out as a family process

There is often a parallel process between a client's disclosure and family processes. Let's expand on a few points.

Coming out as trans was a challenging process for Liam's family. Many families experience less difficulty. A newer trans male client who is 17 told us that his mother "always knew." His family fully accepted and supported him from the start. When he asked his mother why she had never shared her suspicions about his gender, she sagely stated, "You needed to make your own discoveries."

While research on families is in its infancy, studies suggest that family understanding and support significantly affect the well-being of transgender youth (McConnell, Birkett, & Mustanski, 2016). Family support can be a resilience factor for clients at every age.

Lev and Alie (2012) have developed a model for therapeutic work with families. Their model includes the following stages: 1) Learning of the family member's gender nonconformity; 2) Confusion experienced among family members; 3) Negotiating adjustments to be made within the family; and 4) Finding balance, which occurs once the person is accepted and integrated back into the family as their authentic self. We will illustrate these stages through the story of George, a 58-year-old client.

George had a complicated history of treatment prior to seeking our services. George had several negative experiences in prior therapy, and preferred to explore these issues slowly. He had not been in active treatment for about five years.

From an early age, George did not identify as cisgender. The oldest child and the only boy in a family of girls, he (preferred pronoun) enjoyed playing dress-up and house with his sisters. He enjoyed painting his fingernails, and his mother supported these decisions. George's father, a conservative immigrant tradesman, disapproved. His father physically abused him to "make him more of a man." George entered the family business, married, and lived within the gendered norms of the times. His job choice, dress, and family roles felt congruent at times, and incongruent at others. George could be very dominant and sometimes aggressive, but also gentler and more sensitive. George felt confined within the binary of male/female, and questioned whether male was the "correct" gender.

In his prior treatment, George's therapist encouraged experimentation with being feminine and urged him to wear female clothing to sessions. George was initially enthusiastic, and "tried to become Georgeann." Part of the struggle in being Georgeann was how different George's internal and external mirror were. The Georgeann he dreamed about was graceful and feminine. The image in the mirror was stocky, masculine and "unattractive."

A friend from George's support group mentioned having participated in a photo shoot, including professional makeup, hair and glamour shots. George booked a session and emerged with a portfolio of photos of himself as a woman. While the image in these photos were closer to what George had imagined, he was not seeking to become the person in the photos. This created more confusion about who he was and who he wanted to be.

When George entered treatment, he was relieved by the assurance that he did not have to choose a gender or be confined by a binary. George decided not to label himself or his identity. As he settled into a more fluid identity, his anxiety visibly decreased. We explored what would be helpful in terms of coming out to the most important people in his life—his family.

Learning about a family member, and confusion experienced

George's family system consisted of his wife, Allison, to whom he had been married for 25 years, and their two grown-up daughters. This was a second marriage for both George and Allison.

Allison initially entered therapy reluctantly. Mistrust abounded. Allison had discovered George's gender exploration accidentally. She found the glamour shots while searching for something in his dresser. Angry and confused, Allison confronted George about the photos. George refused to answer her questions (which he had still not done). Allison's individual therapist diagnosed the cross-dressing as a sexual paraphilia. This triggered Allison, who was a survivor of childhood abuse. She began to think of George as a "pervert." At the family session she was furious.

George and Allison loved one another, but it was difficult for Allison to let go of being "silenced." With coaxing, they began to explore what George's gender identity meant to him individually and to them as a couple. George disclosed his pain of not fully understanding his gender identity. He shared that even when presented with the glamorous image of what he could look like as a woman, it still did not seem right. He described extreme discomfort in his body. His refusal to talk to Allison was due to shame, and fear of being judged as "less than a man."

Once George was more disclosing, Allison's angry demeanor lessened. Allison was able to express her own fears.

Allison had many worries. Was George keeping other secrets that she would later find out about? Would he want to fully transition at one point, which she saw as an end to the marriage? Would their already diminished sex life end entirely? Allison was fearful about her kids. How would they react if he shared his gender struggles? Would they feel uncomfortable? Would their extended family reject them entirely? George shared that he had many of the same concerns.

Negotiating adjustments and finding balance

Through the course of several sessions the couple discussed George's understanding of his current gender identity. George did not really identify as male or female, but had aspects of both genders. George did not feel "right" in his body did but was working on increased body acceptance.

Even after these explanations, it was difficult for Allison to fully understand George's inner mirror, but she tried. Allison became less reactive to his clothing choices, many of which were actually subtle and more androgynous. Allison recognized that George's gender identity was not a threat to their marriage. Their sex life became stronger as their emotional intimacy increased. In turn, this acceptance led George to hate his body less.

The couple shared George's gender story with their daughters, and were met with acceptance. The kids reacted with respectful curiosity, and were able to be more open about some things they had been holding back, including their own suspicions about George's gender fluidity. George felt fully authentic with Allison and his children.

The couple decided not to share George's gender story with extended family. They did not believe that it would be met with support, and wanted to maintain peace in the remaining years that George's father had left to live. George was at peace with his decision.

Supporting the process/questions to ask

In supporting clients at varying stages in the coming-out process, we have learned a number of lessons about coming out. The primary takeaway is the need to create an environment that is safe and supports sharing while supporting the client's own unique process and gender expression.

The questions below may be helpful to ask in order to shed light on each client's individual process. These can be adapted based on client circumstances and where they are in terms of coming out.

- How do you see yourself? Male/female/both/neither. What is this like?

- At what age did you recognize that your gender identity may be transgender/gender fluid/gender expansive? What do you recall about this time of your life?

- What has it been like coming out to yourself? Others?

- In what ways have you already transitioned? Are these additional types of transition you are considering?

- What body modifications, if any, could be helpful?

- How open are you about your gender identity? At work? At school? At home? With new acquaintances?

- How has your gender identity affected your relationship with your family? Do you feel supported by your family?

- Do you have concerns about body image? Do body-image pressures in the LGBTQ+ community affect you?

- How have you been emotionally affected by coming out/not coming out? What (healthy and unhealthy) things have helped you to cope?

FOR FURTHER EXPLORATION

- Why are secrets unhealthy?

- Are there ways you related to the content in this chapter—and things you have disclosed to others which you knew could be met with a lack of support?

- Create your own circle of support diagram. How is this useful in your own life?

- If you have not already done so (and think the label fits), develop a plan for coming out as a trans ally. What would you need to consider? Who would you come out to?

Chapter 6

Trauma, Identity, and Body Image

Randy is a 22-year-old client, an assigned female at birth whose history illustrates some of the points we want to make in this chapter. Randy originally came to therapy following an unsuccessful semester at college. At that time, Randy dressed in a very feminine manner—skirts and accessories—and had long hair. Randy was binge eating two or three times a day, alternating with restrictive eating. Randy would also cut daily, most predominantly in the chest area. Randy did not understand the reason for restrictive eating or cutting. Randy also alluded to some negative sexual experiences while at college, but stopped short of calling them rape.

Randy was challenging to connect with and did not like talking about subjects that evoked strong feelings. While Randy would express some concerns, such as being "a failure for leaving school" or "hating my body," Randy was unable to elaborate further. Randy was unable to sit with uncomfortable feelings.

After a few months, Randy began to dress more neutrally. Randy described alternating between feeling masculine and feminine. Randy was confused about these feelings. Randy became more engaged in therapy and more able to show emotions, discussing memories of gender dissonance. Randy shared a memory of a dress-up birthday party (hair, nails, fancy clothes) and the discomfort Randy felt.

As Randy settled into a more fluid identity, the binge eating and restrictive eating reduced. Randy began to identify as transgender and stated a preference for he/him pronouns.

Randy's mother, Lisa, scheduled a meeting to provide additional history. Randy's father died shortly before Randy's third birthday. As a child, Randy had childhood cancer. While undergoing treatment, Randy went from a gregarious youngster to one who was more withdrawn.

With puberty, this withdrawal intensified. Randy frequently commented negative on her body, including her large breasts.

Throughout family therapy, Lisa has struggled with names and pronouns.

Randy's story may present a different idea of "trauma" from how some people think of it—medical concerns, the loss of his father. What is your definition of trauma? Perhaps your description includes the idea of an emotionally overwhelming event or a threat of some kind. As you think about examples of trauma, some things that come to mind may include violence, bullying, and discrimination. Clients on the gender-diverse spectrum experience these events at a higher rate or in a more extreme way than other clients.

Trauma, gender identity, and body image are intricately connected. The Sidran Institute, an organization that helps people understand trauma, defines psychological trauma as an event or enduring condition in which a person's ability to integrate emotional experience is overwhelmed or in which the individual experiences a threat to life or bodily integrity. This is the definition of a "Big T" trauma, a deeply disturbing event that reduces a person's sense of control.

One of the things that distinguishes psychological trauma from other distressing events is its effect on the body. According to Bessel van der Kolk, an internationally renowned trauma expert, trauma overwhelms the central nervous system, altering the way people process memories. "Trauma is the current imprint of that pain, horror, and fear living inside people," he says (van der Kolk, 2015, p.53). "After trauma, the world is experienced with a different nervous system that has an altered perception of risk and safety." In van der Kolk's words, "the body keeps the score."

In the professional training sessions we lead, we illustrate the connection between body and trauma. We begin by asking people to do a body scan to sense whether there are any areas of tension and invite them to let go of any tension they may feel. We then ask them to think about a neutral situation, and again scan their bodies for tension. With a neutral cue, the body is generally free of new tension. Next, they consider a more distressing situation, but not a traumatic one, and see if there is any tension in the body. Usually, this scan results in at least one area of the body, such as the stomach, shoulders, or neck, that feels tension and "holds" the distressing situation. When recalling traumas, body responses are even more intense.

What are some examples of trauma? Perhaps you think about the most profound cases: war, natural disasters, physical and sexual abuse, or catastrophic accidents. These are the so-called Big T events, and clients often use them as a yardstick of trauma.

Many of our gender-expansive clients have had Big T traumas, and others have experienced an accumulation of smaller events. "Small T" traumas can have an equal impact, especially when people minimize their own experiences. Examples include being misgendered or teasing. Reminders of their assigned sex, such as a monthly menstrual cycle or the need to shave, can also be traumatic. While Small T traumas do not threaten physical safety, they can leave a person feeling ineffective, defective, or powerless.

When faced with Big T threats, the body and mind's defense systems take over, and people respond in three ways: fight, flight, or freeze. These responses are automatic and protective. For example, a transmasculine client froze when he was surrounded by a group of intoxicated men hurling slurs at him. They eventually stopped and left him alone. This client was initially upset that his response was not "manly" enough, but was able to realize that not engaging with a group of angry men was a safer and wiser response.

Closely related are avoidance responses. While Randy had only limited early memories of his early medical history, Randy's tendency to sidestep feelings (the alexithymia) was an artifact of this early trauma. It is important to validate the utility of the response while emphasizing current safety. Randy had little choice but to shut down when he was young; his mother was grieving and responding to the medical crisis. But there are alternative ways to express feelings. These may include art, journaling, and music, to name a few.

In working with trauma, we draw on a number of sources—van der Kolk's work, as well as the body of literature related to somatic therapies, such as the work of Peter Levine (2008, 2012) and Pat Ogden and Janina Fisher (2015). Levine and Ogden and Fisher focus on the body, particularly sensory experiences that are frozen or trapped by trauma and lead to difficulties with internal self-regulation. Their work helps us to understand why people who have had past traumas feel chronically unsafe and uncomfortable in their bodies, a feeling that may accompany the experience of being in the wrong body. These clients may also be hypervigilant, on high alert. Marti, a trans female client with a history of severe physical abuse, was initially unaware of what triggered her binging. Internally, Marti felt alternately numb and on high alert. Externally, she felt unsafe, and had several awful experiences related to being trans. She was verbally harassed while in a public restroom. This led to fears about using restrooms when she was not at home, which led to painful physical repercussions.

Clients like Marti often struggle with internal interoception—an understanding of what they are feeling in their bodies, including emotions and body cues. They may have difficulty connecting emotions and physical sensations. We often ask clients to focus on their bodies when they are experiencing an emotion, and to identify where they feel this emotion in their bodies. Some people with trauma also experience depersonalization—the sense of being a detached observer. Trans clients describe many of these symptoms, key among them a loss of agency and control.

For a glimpse into how this manifests, consider being born into the wrong body, the trauma of which is something clients can exert only limited control over. One of our trans female clients, Rosy, would have electrolysis treatments to help reduce beard growth. The results were temporary, and when hair growth resumed, she became very depressed. Like Randy, Rosy would become almost mute and have extreme difficulty expressing feelings. Our trans male clients often exhibit similar depression and body dysphoria at the time of their monthly menstrual cycles.

While trauma is common among many clinical populations, it seemingly disproportionately affects those who are most vulnerable. LGBTQ people experience trauma at higher rates than the general population, and they often experience multiple traumas. For people who are gender expansive, these traumas may occur at any point in their development. This can include early trauma, a trauma that accompanies the formative stages of gender development, or events that occur post transition. A question that many clinicians ask during our talks is whether trauma *causes* someone to become transgender. The answer is a resounding no. But trauma can result in depression, and it can affect body image and create significantly greater body dysphoria. According to research by Suliman *et al.* (2009), multiple traumas are associated with high levels of post-traumatic stress disorder (PTSD), anxiety, and depression. Those traumas that are related to gender identity, as in the case of our client Rosy, are felt most keenly.

While many of us need only look at our own caseloads to validate these ideas, a useful resource is *Injustice at Every Turn* (2011), a survey of transgender and gender-nonconforming people (also known as the National Transgender Discrimination Survey, or NTDS). The report highlights the pervasive discrimination, bias and harassment, economic disparity, homelessness, poor health outcomes, and abuse that trans people experience. Trans people who responded to the survey reported "serious acts of discrimination" related to gender identity.

Types of trauma

Gender-diverse people experience many traumas. Such traumas occur within schools, workplaces, homes, and other places that should be safe. These are traumas to and about the body, and traumas that affect the body. Below are some categories of trauma and examples.

Hate violence

Hate- or bias-motivated crimes occur when perpetrators intentionally select victims because of who they are (Marzullo & Libman, 2009)—in this case, because they are in some way identifiable as gender nonconforming. Research shows that transgender people are at elevated risk for physical and sexual assault, harassment, bullying, and hate-crime victimization (McKay, Lindquist, & Misra, 2017). Many transgender people walk through life in states of hypervigilance and fear.

Hate violence is devastating. In a study of 500 transgender people in San Francisco, researchers found that a history of forced sex, gender-based discrimination, and gender-based victimization was associated with attempted suicide (Clements-Nolle, Marx, & Katz, 2006). One factor that plays a role in suicide attempts is how readily a person's physical appearance identifies that person as transgender (Haas, Rogers, & Herman, 2014). Passing, which refers to a person's ability to be regarded at a glance to be either a cisgender man or a cisgender woman, seems to be a protective factor.

Kendra, a transfeminine client in her 50s, demonstrates the challenges associated with hate crimes. Kendra had only recently started dressing femininely. From the outset of therapy, certain life events were "off limits" for discussion. While these events were connected to her anorexia, chronic depression, and suicidality, she could not tolerate talking about them. After some time, she was ready to talk about a trauma in her early 30s. One night she and a friend went dancing. Kendra was wearing a dress and heels and "feeling great." A crowd of intoxicated men surrounded Kendra and her friend. Her friend escaped and was able to summon the police, but Kendra was sexually assaulted. Her rapists called her a "cunt" and told her that they would "show her what women get." A responding police officer remarked that "she should expect this if she tried to fool men." Kendra internalized each aspect of the trauma. Restricting food helped her to numb the pain.

Trans men and women are also at risk of homicide. There have been well-publicized murders, such as Brandon Teena, whose life and death were the subject of the movie *Boys Don't Cry,* and many more that were not memorialized by Hollywood. In 2018, there were 29 documented homicides in the US. Many people die every year for daring to embrace their gender identity.

Being a sex worker is also dangerous for trans people. One of our clients, a police officer in a high-crime urban setting, related the story of a young transgender woman of color, Aisha. As the responding officer at the young woman's homicide, he was shocked at viciousness of the murder. What affected the officer even more was the response of family when he notified them of their daughter's death. Our client sensitively referenced the victim as Aisha, and the family angrily denied that they knew her. They became combative when he switched to Aisha's legal name. The officer later discovered that Aisha was homeless, and that the only way she could earn money was through prostitution.

Bullying and intimidation

Bullying is an aggressive behavior by that involves a power imbalance and is repeated. Bullying may inflict physical, psychological, social, or educational harm (Gladden *et al.*, 2013). Intimidation is an experience that results in fear of injury or harm.

Like hate violence, bullying and intimidation are bias traumas. Gender-expansive youth often feel unsafe in school. Bullying frequently seeps into the home in the form of cyberbullying—the use of electronic communication (text messaging, social media and other online means) to send threats. Cyberbullying is often anonymous, and the lack of an identifiable perpetrator decreases the victim's sense of control and increases their fear. One of our clients would go into a state of panic whenever she heard her phone beep.

Bullying has many negative effects. These include a decline in academic functioning, school refusal, efforts to numb emotions (drugs, alcohol, cutting, eating disorders), and mood disorders. There is also a link between bullying and suicide attempts (Nuttbrock *et al.*, 2014).

Bullying negatively affects mood, self-esteem, and body image, especially when it involves physical appearance. Alyssa was told that a peer would out her if Alyssa did not allow him to cheat on a test. Jasmine, a middle schooler, purchased stimulant drugs to lose weight after peers placed an unflattering photo of her with the word "fugly" on social media. Sean was mockingly referred to by his birth name. Cayden was subjected to repeated taunts of "fag," thrown against lockers, and kicked while in school.

School is not the only place bullying occurs. Andy was a trans male in his mid 20s. His mother frequently commented on the way he dressed, and his grandmother advised him that he would look much prettier with makeup. When he was hospitalized after a suicide attempt, his mother gave him a card addressed, "To My Beautiful Daughter."

Isolation/Exclusion/Rejection

A closely related type of bias is the isolation. Isolation threatens fundamental human needs, such as belonging, self-esteem, and control (Benenson *et al.*, 2011).

Transgender youth are more likely to be excluded by peers because they are "different" (Baum *et al.*, 2012). Social isolation involves feeling emotionally separate from social networks, especially family, or rejection by important individuals in a person's life, such as friends and peers or churches or other religious institutions.

Isolation may result in:

- the need to conceal identity from self or others due to stigma or prevailing gender norms

- lack of accurate information about gender identity, including appropriate role models.

Gender expectations are powerful. When many people think of gender, they think of the gender binary—that gender must be male or female—

and of the societal expectations and norms associated with each. It may be difficult for the average person, parent, or clinician to understand that many people do not identify as male or female but as both or neither, and that their identification can change from day to day. This may also be difficult for clients themselves to understand.

The need to conceal one's identity is more challenging than many who are cisgender understand. If you think of a time when you had a secret that may have been damaging and guarded it fiercely for fear that someone else might discover it, perhaps you have some idea of how it would feel for trans people. This need to protect the secret leads to cognitive isolation and distance from role models and community.

In our office setting, which is shared by people of all identities—gay and straight, trans and cis, binary and nonbinary—we highlight various identities with nonbinary art that does not contain bodies, and with books and magazines celebrating all genders and affectional orientations. A powerful story involves one of our clients, a gay cisgender man in his 70s. He came from a very religious background and even stayed married because he feared what would happen if he revealed that he was gay. On meeting him in the waiting room one day, he was in tears, holding a copy of *Out* magazine. "I can't believe such a thing exists," he said. "I've had to hide who I am. I'm so glad others can be open."

Microaggressions and microassaults

Microaggressions are expressions of indirect, subtle, or unintentional discrimination. Microaggressions can be verbal, behavioral, or environmental. Microassaults, however, are deliberate and explicit. Their intention is to hurt or discriminate, for example denying service to someone who is transgender while saying, "We don't like your kind here."

While microaggressions may be subtle, they are also powerful. Transgender people face microaggressions daily, whether it's a comment or question, a second glance on the street, or a lack of depiction in the magazines. Microaggressions perpetuate the superiority of a cisnormative worldview (Sue, 2010).

Examples of microaggressions include:

- Asking questions out of curiosity rather than necessity (including questions about physical aspects of transitioning)

- Compliments such as "You don't even look trans"

- Qualifying remarks such as "For a trans man, you…"

- Implying there is a reason for trans identity, such as asking, "Are you trans because you were abused?"

- Becoming overly apologetic with slips on name or pronouns.

Randy described his otherwise supportive mother as one who refused to change her cell phone picture of him wearing a flowery bikini. When pressed, she told him, "You'll always be my little girl."

Other examples of microaggressions are related to misgendering. Misgendering is referring to someone using a word, especially a pronoun or form of address, that does not correctly reflect the gender with which they identify—for example, calling a transgender woman "he." Both intentional and unintentional misgendering can be traumatic. Unintentional misgendering often occurs in institutional settings when gender markers or names have not been legally changed. An example of misgendering is when trans students are identified in yearbooks using their birth names, rather than their preferred names. Students also struggle when substitute teachers call the legal name on an attendance roster. This may out them to peers.

For us as clinicians and allies, it can be helpful to reflect on our own experiences. Have you been on the receiving end of microaggressions? How did it feel? People describe a variety of reactions: questioning whether the statement was intentionally hurtful, asking themselves if they have a right to be angry, being depressed or angry. This self-reflection allows us to look at our language, behaviors and the messages we imply, and avoid assumptions. It is also important to foster inclusive and supportive environments.

Body incongruence and betrayals

One important aspect of trauma often neglected in the literature is the trauma associated with being in a body that is incongruent with gender identity. Sometimes people describe this as feeling as if they are in the "wrong" body, or state that they have feel that "something is not right."

People who identify in a more neutral or fluid way may not express this as directly. For them, the trauma may be in being misunderstood or pointedly questioned about other physical presentations or attire. For example, Riley, an agender teen, enjoyed dressing in a way that reflected how they (preferred pronoun) were feeling that day. This ranged from very masculine clothing to flowery tiaras and flowing dresses. This confused Riley's mother no end. Riley was also pointedly stopped in the hallway of their school and asked, "Are you a boy or a girl?" in an aggressive tone.

Clients who identify as transgender report a significant number of traumas, including body betrayals. Randy, for example, felt very angry at developing from a slimmer, more boyish body, to a body that contained larger breasts and curves. Randy would often over bind, using binders that were too small and wearing them much longer than he should. While Randy would ultimately like to have top surgery, his parents would like him to wait until after high school. A colleague of ours uses the term "corrective surgery" with clients. The literal definition, righting something that is wrong, definitely seems to fit here.

Another example can be the trauma of the monthly menstrual cycle, an unwelcome reminder of biology. For some clients, especially those in the exploratory phases of looking at gender identity, this may be difficult and can result in depression. Clinically, this can be a challenge, as clients may be doing well with regard to gender dysphoria until the onset of monthly menses. Clients may express despair, hopelessness, and even suicidal ideation at this time. One of our transmasculine clients, Evan, would do very well three weeks out of the month. With the first sign of his menstrual period, however, there was a marked change and he became very depressed and often cut himself.

When monthly periods cause undue stress, clients wish to discuss options to stop the menstrual cycle with their medical providers. Such options include birth control, although this may be too "feminine" for some people, even if the pills are discreetly placed in a different container. Some people who begin birth control may also have unwelcome breast enlargement. Other trans clients may go on testosterone. What is most important is to help clients see that they have control.

Eating disorders

Throughout this book, we have looked at the connections between body image and gender identity. Eating disorders are commonly seen within the LGBT community. Eating disorders can function as a coping response to trauma. Eating disorders can serve as a way to assert power and control, to dissociate from painful emotions, to express pain, to numb or modulate emotions, and as a means of self-harm.

Power and control

Many people who are gender diverse experience situations in which they feel powerless. When Kendra was brutally assaulted, she felt helplessness and terrified. Restrictive eating allowed her to feel more in control. "Others need to eat. I didn't. I was stronger than all of them." Kendra's healing process was multifaceted; not only did she need to embrace her female self, she also needed to find ways to feel empowered. A key aspect of this was learning martial arts, which increased her sense of power. Kendra also learned that a nourished body is stronger than an emaciated body.

Dissociation

Eating disorders, particularly those on the binge eating spectrum, are remarkably effective at allowing people to dissociate and to escape from emotional pain. Randy binged to avoid feelings connected to his early trauma and to avoid sadness about being in the "wrong body." Keith was bullied at work while transitioning, and binging was the one thing that could take him away completely.

Expressing pain

With the strong connection between alexithymia and trauma, it is not surprising that eating disorders may be a way to express the pain of traumas. Changes in the body are evident. When a client loses a significant amount of weight, this is easily seen by others and can be an indication of emotional pain. Rosy's parents were not open to using her preferred name, and Rosy's anorexia intensified. The visible weight loss helped her parents recognize her pain.

Numbing emotions

Eating disorders can also be a way to numb trauma-related emotions. "If I can stuff myself enough, I can sleep at night," one client reported. Another client used her purging behavior to "numb myself" rather than sit with difficult emotions.

Self-harm

Some clients with trauma feel that they are "bad," and eating disorders can be a form of self-punishment. Kelly, an adult client whose learning disability was only recently diagnosed, was often punished and belittled by her parents due to poor grades. When she came out as transgender, her family rejected Kelly. She often felt like "a failure," and she would restrict food to punish herself, followed by binging. The binging resulted in feeling like a "failure"—a vicious cycle.

Healing trauma, gender identity, and body-image concerns

In working with clients who have a history of trauma, we must address these while concurrently working on body image. The following approaches are especially well suited to working with these traumas and body image, as they do not rely on verbal accounting and instead allow a more somatic form of processing.

Imaginal or visual safe space

Trauma is often overwhelming and therapy should not recreate this. An important starting point for any trauma work is to develop an imaginal safe space. A collage, drawing, or photograph of this place is an excellent starting point. One caveat is that the safe space should not be connected with the trauma in any way. Guided imagery can also be used to help clients to visualize their safe space. Going to this imaginal space can be helpful if the trauma work becomes too intense.

Containment box

Containment boxes are used to contain the pain associated with traumatic memories. To create a containment box, ask the client to select a box (cigar boxes work well) and decorate the outside in any way he/she/they wish that invokes positivity or affirmations of self-care. He/she/they may choose inspirational quotes or images. The inside of the box can contain words, images, and other representations of trauma. Clients can place tangible items inside the box that can serve as a metaphor for aspects of their trauma narrative, offering them the chance to take the items out one at a time for exploration in therapy. Some clients choose to take their box home with them, while others choose to leave the box in our office to access whenever they wish during sessions.

Embodied journaling or poetry

While many people struggle to express feelings, the written word seems to bypass alexithymia. One example is the powerful poetry of Andrea Gibson for inspiration. These mediums can be prompted or unprompted. After people write, clients can be asked to share their journal entries aloud and to notice what they are feeling and experiencing in their bodies.

Examples of prompts include:

- Whether it is the name we were born with, or our chosen name, names often have a story. What is the story of your name? What does your name say about you and your body?

- This is the story my body tells…

- Describe a moment when I felt more empowered in my body.

Mask-making

The idea of masks often resonates with our gender-expansive clients. Masks can be a form of both concealment and protection—a profound metaphor. Masks can also be thought of as representative of the inside/outside aspects of self. Mask-making is sometimes preceded by Charles Finn's 1966 classic poem "Please Hear What I'm Not Saying" (Finn, 2011) which we read out loud. For the mask-making activity, we generally use plain white resin or paper mache masks that clients can decorate as they wish. Masks can relate to any theme that arises during the course of therapy.

Examples of prompts include:

- Create a mask that explores the gender identity you present to the outside world (on the front of the mask) and your inner identity (on the inside of the mask).

- Create a mask that represents cisgender privilege.

- Create a mask that explores how you were following your trauma (on the front of the mask) and prior to your trauma (on the inside of the mask).

Word art

Some clients resist creative expression when they do not believe they have much artistic ability. This exercise is a way to increase creativity while maintaining the safety of the familiar—the written word. To do word art, the client is asked to think of a word or phrase that represents how they are feeling at this moment. Examples include "dysphoric" or "I am not safe." The client then writes/draws the word or phrase in the center of a piece of paper in a way that visually represents its meaning. For example, if the word is "dysphoric," the client may print the word on the page in large letters. Next, they are asked to write as in a journal about the word or phrase. The journal entry wraps around the word or phrase, surrounding it.

Mirror, mirror

This activity is adapted from Hinz (2006) and is an exercise for working with clients who have eating disorders. The client is provided with two pieces of rectangular cardboard (precut) and aluminum foil. They are asked to create and then decorate two "mirrors" in collage style in a way that visually represents positive self-talk and negative self-talk. Once the client has created both mirrors, they share their mirrors with the therapist (or in group if applicable). When ready, the client can destroy the negative mirror to further challenge the negative thoughts.

Examples of prompts include:

- Create a positive/negative mirror that gives voice to your gender/body dysphoria.

- Represent the negative self-talk associated with bullying and the positive self-talk associated with supportive friends or family.

- Create a mirror showing the results of your trauma and the self-care that combats these effects.

FOR FURTHER EXPLORATION

- Think about your definition of trauma before and after reading this chapter. How has it changed? Will this modify how you work with clients?

- Try out one or more of the activities described above—perhaps a combination of art and journaling. What was it like for you? How might this activity be useful for a client who is transgender or has concerns related to body image?

Chapter 7

Challenges for Gender-Expansive Clients

"If I go to treatment, will I have to explain to the others there what it means to be gender nonbinary? Will my therapist know what it means?" (Skylar, a 36-year-old gender-nonbinary client with an eating disorder)

"When I was hospitalized after a suicide attempt, the nursing staff discovered my legal name was different from my preferred name. They misgendered me constantly after that. They used my dead name around other patients, who just looked confused. Why would someone with a female name have a full beard? Several patients who had been friendly toward me changed immediately. One threatened to beat me up if I came near." (Roger, a 21-year-old transmasculine client with bipolar disorder)

"My school counselor said it was 'too difficult' to remember my preferred name and pronouns. She didn't understand why I hated talking to her." (Larry, a 14-year-old transmasculine client in high school)

"When my employer found out I was trans, suddenly I started having 'performance' issues. Leaving too early, nitpicking about reports. It was clear that something had changed, but my increased transparency was the only thing that had." (Mary, a 41-year-old trans woman in financial services)

We hear many stories of the problems our clients encounter within the mental health system and in the world at large. These problems are often connected to misunderstanding and misinformation. The term "minority stress" refers to the many difficulties, such as poor social support, economic pressures, violence, and identity-based discrimination, that marginalized groups often face.

This chapter will examine challenges specific to transgender and gender-expansive clients. Understanding where clients have been before they enter your office will support more effective work with gender-expansive clients.

Injustice at every turn

The previous chapter lays the groundwork for many of the challenges clients may face and describes their often complex histories. Clients frequently have pervasive experiences of mistreatment and discrimination. At times, these stories are so overwhelming it would be easy to think that clients with so many traumas are the outliers. Unfortunately, this is not the case.

In 2011, the National Gay and Lesbian Task Force published *Injustice at Every Turn* (Grant *et al.*, 2011), a survey of 6450 transgender and gender-nonconforming persons. The report highlighted numerous challenges this community faces. Additionally, it demonstrated the impact of anti-transgender bias. Those who were surveyed experienced inequities and violence, resulting in mental health concerns and leading to suicide attempts.

The National Center for Transgender Equality conducted a follow-up survey, the *2015 US Transgender Survey* (USTS) (James *et al.*, 2016), which added to the findings of the original survey. The survey captured responses from more than 27,700 participants from all 50 states, the District of Columbia, Puerto Rico, Guam, American Samoa, and US military bases overseas. Disturbing patterns of mistreatment and discrimination continued to be visible and ever-present.

Neither report mentions or provides information on eating disorders—a key omission, given the close connection between body-image concerns and eating disorders.

Key findings from the 2015 report are presented in the box below. As you read through them, think about how experiences of discrimination, mistreatment, and violence may affect a client's physical and mental health. How do these experiences complicate existing mental health conditions? How can they contribute to body-image concerns and eating disorders?

Some key findings from the *2015 US Transgender Survey*

Discrimination and mistreatment in healthcare:

- One third of those who saw a healthcare provider had negative experiences related to being transgender. Participants reported being verbally harassed or refused treatment because of their gender identity.

- Approximately 60 percent did not seek healthcare, either because of fear of being mistreated or inability to afford treatment.

Pervasive mistreatment and violence:

- More than three-quarters experienced some form of mistreatment in school, including verbal harassment and physical and sexual assault. Approximately 20 percent reported leaving school as a result of the severe mistreatment.

- Nearly half reported being sexually assaulted in their lifetime.

- Nearly half were verbally harassed for being transgender.

- One in ten people experienced violence from an immediate family member because of being transgender.

- Approximately 30 percent reported being fired, denied promotion, and verbally, physically, or sexually assaulted while at work because of gender identity.

Intersectionality—gender identity, race, immigration status, etc.:

- Transgender and gender-diverse people of color had staggering poverty rates: Latino (43%), American Indian (41%), multiracial (40%), and black (38%).

- Undocumented respondents were more likely to face severe economic hardship and violence than other respondents. Nearly one quarter (24%) reported being physically attacked in the previous year. Half said they had been homeless at times in their lifetimes, and 68 percent reported intimate-partner violence.

While many clinicians recognize that gender-expansive people encounter discrimination, seeing the actual statistics is sobering. At our presentations, clinicians commonly have such stories to share. They describe their clients' experiences of discrimination and violence, and also the effects of gender identity when combined with minority race, immigration status, or disability. If you are unfamiliar with the idea of intersectionality, please check out the writings of poets such as Sonia Guiñansaca, a queer woman of color. Her poetry is powerful and takes on topics such as violence against women and children, poverty and economic hardship, immigration status, and prejudicial treatment of gender-diverse people.

Guiñansaca's poetry and the research illustrate the reality of gender-based inequities. How do these things affect a client's physical and mental health? How do intersectional identities, such as race, immigration status, and disability, come into play?

The survey statistics are alarming, though not surprising. They parallel client stories—stories of harassment at school, of rejection by family members, of suicide attempts; stories of anxiety about being misgendered in public settings, of mistreatment when seeking medical assistance; stories of being outed in the workplace, of being fired for a minor offense after employers learn that clients are transgender. And stories of intense reactions to news articles featuring transphobia or the murder of another transgender person.

It is impossible to separate the impact of discrimination and mistreatment from a discussion about mental and physical health. As the examples below show, it is rare that we meet someone who is gender expansive whose mental health is not affected by minority stress.

Tara, a 23-year-old trans woman, entered therapy during an episode of crippling depression and bulimic symptoms. She struggled to get out of bed each day, shower, dress, and leave the house. Three months before entering therapy, she quit her job after being severely verbally harassed by co-workers. Her fears of being harassed (or worse) prevented her from applying for new jobs. Tara's depression spiraled after she lost her sense of worth and purpose, propagating a disastrous cycle. Her depression and eating disorder contributed to her continued unemployment. Her unemployment contributed to her depression and bulimia.

Julien, a 20-year-old gender-nonbinary client, struggled to remain sober after completing substance abuse treatment. They (preferred pronoun) were unable to find recovery housing that would accept them as a nonbinary individual. They were uncomfortable in most 12-step meetings and struggled to find a sponsor. Within weeks of discharge, Julien wound up homeless and relapsed. Julien's drug use was a way to cope and to find housing through substance-use treatment programs.

Challenge: History of gender-based discrimination, violence and mistreatment

Tara and Julien are like many clients who come to us already having had significant negative life experiences. How do we begin to counteract their history of mistreatment? How do we help clients like Tara and Julien know that we are safe and trustworthy?

Meyer's Minority Stress Model describes how daily life as a member of a marginalized community can impact overall health and wellness. The model suggests that members of sexual or gender minority groups experience multiple prejudicial encounters. This stress leads to psychological concerns, including chronic depression, anxiety, and substance abuse (Meyer, 2003). Transgender-affirmative practices recognize and respond to these challenges while simultaneously focusing on client strengths and resiliency.

The Gender Minority Stress and Resilience (GMSR) measure is a helpful tool to assess client experiences with minority stress. This model, adapted by Testa *et al.* (2017), assesses external and internal stressors associated with a person's status as a gender minority. It also measures minority resilience factors that positively influence mental health.

According to the measure, transgender and gender-expansive individuals are influenced by seven stressors, four of which are external: gender-based victimization; gender-based rejection; gender-based discrimination; and identity non-affirmation (i.e., being misgendered). The other three are internal: negative expectations for future events; internalized transphobia; and nondisclosure of one's identity (hiding gender identity status to protect one's self or others). The model also describes two resiliency factors—community connectedness and pride in one's identity—that positively contribute to transgender adjustment.

Our clients experience a combination of the factors described above. These are often related to navigating gender-minority identities. Our role is to: 1) recognize and respond to the trauma and negative thinking patterns that result from transphobic experiences, and 2) increase resilience by supporting coping strategies and by magnifying personal strengths.

Donnie, a 32-year-old African-American trans male client, has worked with us for several years. He sought therapy to manage his anxiety and binge eating. Donnie noticed a connection between spending time with his religiously conservative family and his binging. Donnie's mother refused to acknowledge his name and pronouns and consistently spoke of the "sin" involved with his identity. He often left family gatherings feeling powerless and overwhelmed. The stress associated with these feelings resulted in his binge eating. Despite this, Donnie does not want to break ties completely with family. Our treatment has focused on affirming these challenges, supporting Donnie in setting better boundaries with his family, and helping him to develop concrete coping skills to be able to manage necessary family encounters.

External stressors: victimization, rejection, discrimination, and identity non-affirmation

As you read our clients' stories, consider how such histories will affect your work with clients. How are eating disorder and other symptoms a manifestation of these traumas? What negative cognitions could arise from these experiences? How will you support increased resilience?

Many of the stressors we've discussed are external stressors—forces outside a person's control that create anxiety, shame, or other difficult emotions. External stressors are difficult for a number of reasons. Compared with internal stressors, they are much more difficult to control. When combined with identity stress and disclosure of a trans or expansive identity, the effects of the stress multiply.

One of our clients most severely affected by disclosure of his trans identity was Marshall, a 27-year-old transmasculine client. Marshall entered therapy with bulimia and post-traumatic stress disorder. These symptoms were intricately connected to his transition. Marshall experienced multiple instances of violence during the early stages of coming out. The most profound was a rape by a classmate, who became enraged after learning that Marshall was transgender. While he was ultimately able to work through the trauma, the fact that the rape was connected to his trans identity made the work all the more challenging.

While not all clients have stories as traumatic as Marshall's, many of them experience discrimination and rejection, which also have negative effects. Notably, many of these experiences occur within institutions that are meant to provide or support therapy, such as 12-step communities or school counseling centers.

Our client Julien, was unable to engage fully in 12-step communities and unable to find sponsors or groups that understood his trans identity. He often felt uncomfortable attending meetings and was aware of second glances and whispering among others in attendance.

Gender-based discrimination includes difficulty obtaining employment, housing, medical care, and legal documents because of gender identity. Albert, a 40-year-old transmasculine client with a long-term eating disorder, was not allowed to enter a local treatment program because the facility was unable to accommodate his housing needs. The program placed him on a waiting list for weeks before admitting that it had no intention of admitting someone who was transgender. He was eventually admitted to a general psychiatric hospital, where staff were not trained to monitor or treat the eating disorder.

Of all the external stressors our clients experience, the most damaging is identity non-affirmation. Identity non-affirmation, or misgendering, occurs when others intentionally or unintentionally refer to a person or use language to describe a person that does not align with their gender identity. Larry, for example, is the 14-year-old trans male student quoted at the beginning of the chapter. He was required to meet with the school guidance counselor after he was discovered purging at school. The guidance counselor refused to use Larry's preferred name and pronouns in sessions and dismissed Larry's concern when Larry tried to correct her.

Internal stressors: negative expectations of future, internalized transphobia, and nondisclosure of identity

Thus far, we have looked at our clients' experiences in navigating their gender journeys. Internal stressors are factors that reside within the client, based on what they have internalized as a result of negative life experiences.

For instance, clients who have experienced discrimination, prejudice, and social rejection often develop expectations that this will be the outcome of all similar situations. Such negative beliefs and expectations stem from general societal stigma against gender-diverse people. Tara, for example, has doubts about her ability to find a job that will not include prejudice from others. This self-limiting belief stops her from taking steps to find employment. Julien, who does not believe there is a place for them in the 12-step community, struggles to envision themself in long-term recovery or finding any supports whatsoever.

A common phenomenon is internalized transphobia. Internalized transphobia occurs when the person takes in the negative societal attitudes toward gender-expansive people. For example, Tonya, a 17-year-old trans woman questioning her (preferred pronoun) gender identity, came to us for therapy after her parents discovered cuts on her arms and legs. After several sessions, Tonya disclosed a significant sense of self-hate. She used derogatory and offensive language to describe herself, her gender identity, and her body. She cut herself to punish her body and in a desperate attempt to silence her mind.

Hiding one's trans identity is another common internal stressor. While hiding gender identity status is often an effort to protect oneself from harm, it takes a significant internal toll. Roger, the 21-year-old trans male client with bipolar disorder who was quoted at the beginning of this chapter, has been hospitalized several times for suicide attempts. Roger does not disclose that he is transgender when he enters a hospital, having had multiple prior experiences of discrimination and violence. Despite his efforts to conceal his identity, a member of the nursing staff outed him during his most recent hospital stay by calling him by his legal name. This further intensified his mistrust in healthcare systems.

Challenge: Overcoming the *Diagnostic and Statistical Manual of Mental Disorders* and historical prejudice

Lily, a 15 year-old transfeminine client with social anxiety and bulimia, struggles to connect with her (preferred pronoun) psychiatrist. While collaborating with us on the case, the doctor shared his doubts about Lily's gender identity. The psychiatrist told Lily's parents that "he" (misgendering Lily) must have had a trauma of some kind and that this was clearly a trauma response. When Lily denied that there was any trauma and attempted to reaffirm her gender identity, the psychiatrist told her that they would need to work on getting to the root of the resistance. The receipt for the visit listed two diagnoses: gender identity disorder and oppositional defiant disorder.

Tyson is a 32-year-old trans male with severe depression. Tyson feels that his previous providers over-focused on the fact that he was transgender in identifying the reason for his depression. Tyson disagreed. One provider asked him for his "real name." Tyson's depressive symptoms increased with each experience.

Some providers continue to perpetuate the stereotype that transgender and gender-expansive clients are inherently unwell. While the scenarios described above are thankfully no longer the norm, they still occur. Collectively, however, our thinking as a profession about gender expansiveness has shifted considerably—from a pathologizing approach to a much more affirming stance.

Before 2013 and for more than 30 years, people who entered therapy questioning or exploring their gender identity were given a diagnosis of gender identity disorder. This diagnosis presumed that the cross-gender identification was a mental illness. There was also an assumption that clients with gender identity disorder were inherently depressed because they were transgender, when depression can be caused by any number of factors. The definition also reinforced the binary gender system. Nonbinary clients were not represented in this description—erasing their experience altogether.

In 2013, *Diagnostic and Statistical Manual of Mental Disorders 5*[1] revised this diagnosis to "gender dysphoria"—focusing on the *distress* associated with gender incongruence (being born into the wrong body) rather than simply having an incongruent gender identity. This focus on body distress was a critical change. Not only has it resulted in less stigma for many of our clients, it has also allowed us to focus on specific ways of changing the body. Clients can be affirmed that their identity as gender-expansive people is not the problem. This shifts the focus instead to the difficulties associated with being born into the wrong body. Refer to the current *DSM* criteria for gender dysphoria for more information.

---

1   *The Diagnostic and Statistical Manual of Mental Disorders (DSM)* is published by the American Psychiatric Association (APA) and offers a common language and standard criteria for the classification of mental disorders.

Under the former categorization, therapists would frequently work with clients to understand the origins of their "identity disturbances," akin to the reactions of Lily's psychiatrist. While many therapists provided supportive counseling that was affirmative to clients, this was not always true. Gender identity disorder was sometimes used to rationalize harmful practices to "correct" the transgender identity—similar to conversion therapies for sexuality. Similarly, we are learning of a diagnosis called "rapid-onset gender dysphoria." Some clinicians are beginning to adopt this diagnosis, which implies that adolescents with gender dysphoria are going through a developmental "phase." This is not a formal diagnosis and can be a way of dismissing gender exploration.

Gender dysphoria

The core concept behind changing the diagnosis from gender identity disorder to gender dysphoria centers on depathologizing the transgender experience. It supports the idea that emerging gender identity and gender exploration is a normal part of human development. Gender identity can develop on many different trajectories—cisgender, gender diverse, and transgender. Gender dysphoria describes the distress caused by the gender incongruence. The key distinction is that gender diversity itself is not a mental disorder. Gender dysphoria acknowledges the presence of clinically significant distress in several areas of functioning, including school, social, and occupational interactions.

Gender dysphoria focuses on the client's strong identification with their non-assigned gender. This can include preferring clothing or toys associated with the non-assigned gender or a desire to have body features of the non-assigned gender.

To show how gender dysphoria can present in a client, let us consider George.

George is a 42-year-old trans man (assigned female at birth) with binge eating. George knew from early childhood that he was not supposed to be a girl. George recalls playing with boys' toys, dressing in boys' clothes, and telling his elementary teachers that he was going to be a man when he grew up. At puberty, George felt betrayed by his body as it developed breasts. He tried to ignore the incongruence he felt over the next 30 years, but could not shake the feeling of being in the wrong body. This affected his ability to navigate social and work situations, and it contributed to family discord. While George often fantasized about beginning hormone replacement therapy and obtaining surgeries to become more masculine, he did not believe it was possible for him to transition at this stage of his life.

With time, George was able to take steps toward transitioning. He started hormone replacement therapy and began to feel more "himself." George went forward with top surgery as well. This was the most affirming, rewarding moment of his life. George's binge eating decreased with each step he took toward aligning his body with his gender identity.

Treatment for gender dysphoria focuses on taking measures to alleviate body-related distress. This includes having a space to talk about feelings and socially or medically transitioning.

While the majority of our clients struggle with gender dysphoria, it is important to note that many gender-expansive and transgender individuals do not. Gordon, for example, is both a trans man and a therapist. He is well adjusted and has no dysphoria connected to his male identity. Gordon and his wife have been in couples counseling to work on improving communication. There would be no reason to diagnose Gordon with gender dysphoria.

Challenge: Mental health difficulties

The *US Transgender Survey* highlights alarming rates of mental health issues in the transgender and gender-expansive community. Approximately 40 percent of respondents said they experienced serious psychological stress, compared with 5 percent of the US population. The suicide rate in the transgender community is nine times greater than the national average. Transgender clients with disabilities and transgender people of color have an even greater risk of suicide (James *et al.*, 2016).

These responses mirror what we see in practice. A significant number of gender-expansive clients experience suicidal ideation, depression, self-harm, anxiety, substance use disorders, and, of course, eating disorders. This is related to the combination of gender-minority stressors and the impact of navigating gender/body dysphoria.

Jared, whom you met in the introduction, is a good example of how gender identity struggles can result in suicidal thoughts and attempts.

When Jared, who was assigned female at birth, told his family that he identified as a boy, they were not supportive. He was met with a similar lack of acceptance from friends. Feeling alone and as if he was a burden to family and friends, Jared overdosed on his medication. This was the first of several suicide attempts. Jared felt as if there was no way out. If he denied how he felt, he was destined to live inauthentically. If he embraced his identity, his family and friends would disapprove. These kinds of dilemmas are common and difficult.

While not all clients attempt suicide, many do harm themselves in other ways. Thirteen-year-old Blair was just beginning to come into his male identity. He was a target of bullies within his school. Blair coped with transphobic comments by cutting his chest, making a small mark for each hurtful comment or instance of misgendering. Blair specifically chose his chest as the area he cut as it reflected the female body he was trying to escape.

Charleen, a 42-year-old trans female client, experienced significant social anxiety despite her recent transition and breast augmentation. While she was more comfortable in her body, she still worried about being "outed" as trans. When she ran into an old friend, the friend laughingly asked if she was going to a masquerade party. When Charleen told the friend she was trans, she was met with shocked silence. Charleen has avoided social gatherings since. She is working to increase her comfort with social situations.

Gender-expansive people misuse addictive substances as a way to cope. Mateo is a 31-year-old Latino transgender client who has just started the coming-out process. He is not out at work, fearing rejection, and presents as feminine in the workplace. He copes with his feelings about this by drinking. Mateo's doctor will not consider medical transition until his alcohol use is under control. While he is motivated for recovery, the alcohol is the only thing that takes away the feelings of dysphoria, and abstinence has been an uphill battle.

Eating disorders are an area of emerging research. There is increased awareness among clinicians of the connection between gender dysphoria and disordered eating behaviors. We will discuss body image concerns and eating disorders in the next chapter.

Challenge: Lack of awareness about trans-affirmative practices

This challenge shifts away from the client experience and returns to the professionals working with transgender and gender-expansive individuals. Think back to your graduate programs. Was there a course that discussed best practices in working with gender-minority clients? Did your internship sites or supervisors prepare you for providing therapy to this clientele? What type of continuing education training, if any, have you received regarding this community?

For many professionals, the answer is "very little" to "none."

When we started to see more transgender and gender-expansive clients seeking therapy, we needed to expand our knowledge. We researched trans-affirmative best practices and networked with other providers engaged in helping the LGBTQ community. These connections and their willingness to share resources and experiences have enriched our work.

Providing a safe, trans-affirmative space for our clients is important. How can you communicate your support throughout therapy? How can you demonstrate inclusivity within your existing methods of treatment? How would a transgender client know that you take a trans-affirmative approach to therapy?

From intake forms to our initial client meetings, we weave inclusive language into all aspects of our practice. We enter the therapy space in a gender-neutral way, not making assumptions. We ask clients about difficult life experiences and their contributions to psychological symptoms. Here are some examples.

- We open all therapy groups by asking participants to share their names and preferred pronouns. Group members are free to explore gender, trying out different names and pronouns as they gain an understanding of their identities. This also gives gender-fluid clients permission to express themselves as they like at any given group meeting. Chris, for example, discovered that he preferred "he/him" pronouns by trying out several gender neutral options before landing on the masculine pronouns.

- We frequently use the expressive arts in our therapy sessions. Our collection of magazines includes options with diverse representation, such as *Curve* and *The Gay Journal*.

- When we developed a short-term trauma group for survivors of sexual violence, we discussed the benefits of a gender-specific space. The goal was to balance inclusivity with the need to accommodate those wishing for a same-gender group. The group was open to any "female-identified" client—language that welcomed cisgender and transgender women alike.

Many of these ideas stem from training sessions and resources specific to providing services to the transgender and gender-expansive community. Many professional organizations host events on this topic, given the increased visibility of the clients. The sense of community and empowerment at these events is phenomenal. It reminds us that gender-expansive people are resilient despite the challenges.

Resiliency factors

Artist Wriply Bennet, a trans woman of color, has been instrumental in developing the Transgender Day of Remembrance, a day in which to remember trans people lost to violence and hate crimes. Bennet states: "…we also stand up, get off of our knees, and do the work for future trans people…to be visible, resilient, and constantly moving forward for a brighter and stronger future" (Tandy, 2015). Bennet's voice reminds clinicians that trans people can combat the wrongs they have encountered in the world.

In the Gender Minority Stress and Resilience measure, Testa and colleagues identified two resiliency factors that contribute to the overall health and well-being of transgender and gender-expansive clients: (1) community connectedness and (2) pride (in transgender or gender-expansive identity).

Community connectedness refers to the degree to which someone associates with other members of their identity group. This could be through social media and virtual resources, or through support groups for transgender and gender-diverse clients. Most of our adolescent clients follow transgender "You-Tubers," as well as using Twitter, Instagram, and Tumblr to connect with others. Larry, the 14-year-old transmasculine client with the less-than-affirming guidance counselor, participates in transgender support groups. Larry has flourished over the last few months. He connected with other transgender teens who share similar experiences with teachers, guidance counselors, and coaches. While he still struggles with depression, he feels less alone and less isolated in his experiences.

Pride is a sense of identity-based confidence and empowerment. Cameron, a 17-year-old transmasculine client in therapy for anorexia, describes attending his (preferred pronoun) first pride event as a turning point in his recovery. Throughout the event, he was correctly gendered—increasing his confidence in his post-treatment body. He recalls facing "fear foods" at the event with minimal discomfort as he was more interested in participating in the celebration than listening to the voice of his eating disorder.

Austin and Craig (2015) note the importance of clients creating a self-generated definition of self, embracing their intrinsic self-worth, having awareness of oppression, connecting with a supportive community, developing hope for the future, engaging in social activism, and being a positive role model for others. We couldn't agree more.

FOR FURTHER EXPLORATION

- Very few people have not been through some form of discrimination, rejection, or harassment. If this is true for you, consider how you have connected to the content of this chapter and to the experiences of our gender-expansive clients. How have these experiences been pivotal in your life? How have you overcome them?

- As community connectedness and pride in one's identity serve as resiliency factors for members of the transgender and gender-expansive community, it is important to be aware of local resources for connecting clients within this community. Take a few minutes to look up local support and therapy groups for transgender individuals, as well as pride festivities. Jot these down so you have them on hand as a reference for future clients.

Chapter 8

Eating Disorders, Gender Identity, and Minority Stress

The following exercise is grounded in clients' descriptions of their experiences.

Settle in, and know that this may bring up some feelings. You can always stop, pause, or breathe. Close your eyes and visualize your body as if you were looking in a mirror. Notice the physical attributes you see on a daily basis. Be especially aware of the more gendered features of your body, such as the shape of your face or your wider or narrower torso. Notice the size of your hips, the length or style of your hair. Move your eyes lower to take in your genitals and note what you see. And now, assign yourself a label. Perhaps the label is "male," "female," or something else. Is this your desired body? If not, what would you like to change?

And now, visualize something new. See the gendered features that you just noticed rearrange themselves in a different way. Play with this. Perhaps your face takes on features generally associated with a sex you were not assigned at birth. Maybe your face is broader (or narrower), your torso stockier (or slimmer), your hips more tapered (or wider). Perhaps you see genitals that you were not born with. How does this feel? Notice the emotions this brings up. Were the feelings positive, seeing the new you with delight? Or were they negative, seeing the new you with dread? Did it feel right or wrong? Imagine yourself moving through a typical day with this new body. What may change about your life? Were these changes positive? Negative? Neutral? What would happen if you were stuck in this imagined body?

And now return to your current self.

This exercise brings up many different responses and emotions, ranging from positive feelings about novelty and change to more negative feelings (anger, sadness, lack of control). This is especially true when people are asked what it would be like to remain in this body. While this brief exercise pales in comparison with what many of our clients experience daily, it helps people to understand a little about what transgender people often face.

Many of our clients relate to the mirror analogy. They describe an internal mirror in which they may see a body that is congruent with their gender identity, and an external mirror that differs significantly. It can get complicated. Consider Dawson, a 19-year-old transgender woman. Dawson, who was in the initial stages of understanding her gender identity, spent many hours each day fantasizing about the body she wished for: slim but curvy, feminine, petite. Dawson's natural body type was larger, broader, and "too masculine." Dawson's eating disorder initially began as an attempt to achieve the desired slender body. Like many people with eating disorders, Dawson's restrictive eating ultimately led to binging. Dawson then began to purge to compensate. It was a vicious cycle of restricting, binging, and purging, which only increased her shame.

Throughout this book, the connection between the body and gender identity is a major theme. When the physical body is at odds with gender identity, eating disorders may ensue. Dawson's struggles reflect some of the broader themes connected to body and gender, as well as the interconnections between categories of eating disorders.

Among gender-expansive clients, eating disorders include:

- *Anorexia*—characterized by restrictive eating or by limiting food choices or groups. People with anorexia may have bodies that are underweight or have a low fat composition, leading to cessation of the menstrual cycle in assigned females.

- *Bulimia*—characterized by binging and compensatory purging behaviors (vomiting, laxative abuse, exercise).

- *Binge eating disorder*—characterized by binging behaviors but no compensatory behavior.

- *Other specific food and eating disorders*—can include a range of disorders, including muscle dysmorphia, in which a person "bulks up" and focuses on muscularity. This also includes "atypical anorexia," in which people eat restrictively but are not weight-compromised, and "atypical bulimia," in which people may purge but not binge. This category encompasses subclinical disordered eating behaviors.

Think back now to the exercise at the beginning of the chapter. If you were struggling with the idea that your body was too large or small to fit gender norms, or if you were obsessing that your body was incongruent with your gender, how would you correct this? Would your options be different if you knew your family would not support you? Or if you were a minor? Like many of our clients, you might develop disordered eating behaviors.

We suggest including at least some questions on gender identity in eating disorder assessments. Conversely, you can ask clients who present for support around gender identity questions about body image and eating-disorder symptoms.

This chapter will explore the "why" of eating disorders among people who are gender expansive, focusing on the functions that eating disorders serve. Chapter 9 will discuss best practices and treatment.

What does the research say?

Prior to becoming specialists in gender identity, our passion was in treating eating disorders. Body-image research contains only limited information devoted to gender-expansive people. Similarly, the research literature on gender identity and eating disorders is sparse, and existing studies often look at the LGBT community as a whole. Being born into an incongruent body is a unique and difficult experience, and it is important to look at the intersection of gender identity and disordered eating.

This lack of knowledge places clients who are gender expansive at risk. Disordered eating and its related symptoms, such as binge eating, purging, and restrictive dieting, are debilitating. They are associated with significant morbidity and with death (Crow *et al.*, 2012).

Current research suggests that transgender people are more likely than cisgender people to have been diagnosed with an eating disorder or to engage in disordered eating (Guss *et al.*, 2016; Watson, Veale, & Saewyc, 2017) and to have body dissatisfaction (van de Grift *et al.*, 2016a). A large-scale study of transgender college students examined associations between gender identity or sexual orientation and eating disorders, finding that a substantial number had engaged in practices such as use of diet pills, laxatives, or vomiting (Diemer *et al.*, 2018). Women (but not men) who reported "gender-identity conflict" engaged in more disordered eating behaviors than cisgender women without gender-identity conflict (Ålgars, Santtila, & Sandnabba, 2010).

These studies have their limitations and are confounded by several factors: sexual orientation as a variable; small population sizes; or single-case studies. Some of the research is qualitative, which can provide a rich description of why transgender people develop eating disorders and body-image concerns (Ålgars *et al.*, 2010; Gordon *et al.*, 2016).

From these studies and our own clinical observations, we can draw some conclusions:

- There are associations between expansive identities, body-image difficulties, and eating disorder behaviors.

- Stresses associated with being gender expansive and experiences of trauma increase vulnerability to eating disorders and body-image difficulties.

- The internal struggle to accept gender-identity differences is a factor in some eating disorders.

- Transgender/expansive people may use weight loss to suppress secondary sexual characteristics and interrupt puberty.

- Weight gain may be a way of bulking up (increasing masculinity).

- Weight loss may be a way to achieve a slimmer body (increasing femininity or achieving boy-like features).

- Disordered eating behaviors can be used to decrease or accentuate gendered features.

- Body-image ideals create increase risk of eating disorders. Striving for weight loss can be a way to conform to ideals of slimness or attractiveness, which assist in passing.

Body and self
Body image as a continuum

> I remember, as a child, lying in my bed at night praying that I would wake up the next day and be a girl, to be my authentic self, and to just have my family be proud of me. I remember looking into the mirror struggling to say just two words: "I'm transgender." (McBride, 2018, p.10)

This quote by Sarah McBride, a well-known transgender activist, captures the connection between body and self. Seeing a physical image that deviates from the authentic self can cause people to try to change the body in unhealthy ways. While that was not Sarah's journey, it is the path that many of our clients traverse before finding healthier ways to attain body acceptance.

In the Body Image chapter (Chapter 3), you learned that body image contains a number of components. These include body-related self-perceptions and self-attitudes—thoughts, beliefs, feelings, and behaviors (Cash, 2011). All of these factors influence body image.

In looking at body image, a helpful tool is the Body Image Continuum (Arizona Board of Regents, 1997). It was developed by researchers at the University of Arizona for use with cisgender people, but is equally relevant for people who are gender expansive. While it is a generalization, often when people have not transitioned socially or medically, they place themselves further to the right side of the continuum. As people change their bodies in healthy ways, such as transition, they tend to place themselves on the left end of the continuum (body acceptance or ownership).

People who change the body in unhealthy ways—such as through disordered eating—often think that it will bring them to body acceptance or ownership, but this is not the case. They tend to be more body-obsessed, have distorted body image, or dissociate from their bodies.

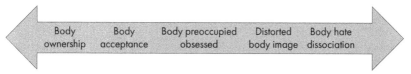

Developed by the Arizona Board of Regents, 1997.

Figure 8.1: The Body Image Continuum

Take a moment to think about this continuum and where you would place yourself. Where would you be, right now, in this moment? If you identify on the right side of the continuum, what would it take to move from where you are to a place of more acceptance?

While body image is relatively stable, there can be some variability. For example, we've had clients whose eating disorders stabilize, or who begin to socially transition and progress to a more accepting body image. There can be days or events, however, that do affect body image. A common one is when our trans male clients menstruate. John, a 15-year-old client who was initially very preoccupied with his body, had transitioned socially and was dressing in ways that were comfortable and felt consistent with his gender identity. He felt more accepting of his body most days of the month. When he was premenstrual or was menstruating, this positive body image would disappear and he would often describe feeling "enormous" and "bloated." Post-menses, his body image would return to a more positive place. Although his family was not yet ready to allow him to take medication to stop the menstrual cycle, this significant change in body image was powerful evidence of the utility of such an approach. Similarly, invalidating environments can affect body image across the board, even when clients have generally good body image.

While the idea of body ownership ("My body is fine—it is mine and I am not influenced by societal views") may not always be possible, it is the aspiration. Several of our clients, including a number who identify as nonbinary, have been successful in actively rejecting the gender-binary and gendered views of body.

The continuum and gender-expansive clients

These continuum examples begin our discussion of why clients with expansive identities use disordered eating to change the body. Gender-expansive clients may be at any place on the continuum.

Body hate/dissociation

Clients who present with body hate and dissociation may be in the early stages of coming out to themselves and to others or may have experienced trauma to or about the body. While these are the most common factors associated with body hate/dissociation, clients can be at this phase of body image at any point in their gender journeys.

In addition to disordered eating, clients with body hate/dissociation may also have self-harm behaviors. Consider 23-year-old Skyler, who was a binge eater. Skyler hated his (preferred pronoun) more petite and feminine body and would cut his breasts and thighs, specifically targeting these as body parts that "outed" him. At times, he described finding cuts on his body but not fully recalling having harmed himself, which is a form of dissociation.

Distorted body image

While clients who identify as transgender or gender diverse may have distorted body image in a classic sense (e.g., a thin person thinking "I'm too fat"), this is generally less the case. Distortions look different. Clients who are trans are not distorted in the idea that they have body parts that conflict with their internal identity.

Projection

This explains how body-image distortions look in gender-expansive clients. Projection is the idea that feelings and emotions can be mis-attributed to a particular body part. In many trans clients, body distortions occur after particular events connected to identity. Misgendering, discrimination, and interpersonal conflict, for instance, may lead to projection and result in body distortion.

For example, Jonathan (preferred name) was a client who was in the beginning stages of exploring a more masculine gender identity. Jonathan's boss required him to wear a name tag with his dead name while at work. By contrast, several co-workers could wear name tags containing nicknames. Jonathan was quite angry, and would often describe feeling "bigger" after work.

Juana, a 35-year-old transfeminine client who has been in treatment with us since her late 20s, also demonstrates this idea.

At the time Juana sought treatment, she struggled with restrictive eating. Using principles of intuitive eating, Juana had worked hard to overcome the restricting and would describe a generally positive body image. Part of that was Juana's acceptance that while her body may not be "classically feminine," social transition and healthy self-care were preferable to a state of chronic illness and starvation.

While Juana placed herself at "body acceptance" on the continuum, there were times when her body image would shift. Most often, this occurred at those times when she was misgendered, especially at family gatherings. Following such incidences, Juana would see herself as "gross" and "huge," and she would slide back into dieting behaviors. Making the connection between stressful situations and projection on the body was helpful. "I need to go on the Keto diet" became a cue to ask herself what had triggered the perceptions of "gross."

Body preoccupied/obsessed

Gender-expansive clients who are body preoccupied/obsessed may show excessive concern about appearance. Such preoccupations can sometimes be reminiscent of body dysmorphic disorder. Lennon, a trans male client who had a smaller frame and height, would often discuss fears that his stature would "out" him to others. He became an avid bodybuilder, eating only protein and spending hours in the gym each day bulking up.

Body acceptance

Clients who demonstrate body acceptance have a generally positive overall body image, and are more accepting of their own bodies. Jael, a transfeminine client who has socially and medically transitioned, has worked hard to accept her body. While there are days when she feels more "bulky" than others, she has been able to take conscious steps to enjoy her natural athleticism. Varied eating and exercise are healthy parts of Jael's daily routine.

Body ownership

Clients who are at the stage of body ownership also have a positive overall body image and the sense that their body (and others' bodies) is fine as is. They do not go to extremes to change the body and do not buy in to societal views of the body. Ramsey, a nonbinary client, has taken conscious steps to change their (preferred pronoun) body in ways that feel good, including top surgery. Ramsey also dresses in a gender-neutral way. Ramsey has reached the point of "amusement" when others stare or question their gender. Self-care, such as eating well, sufficient rest, and a yoga practice, complements Ramsey's body confidence.

Functions of disordered eating

Eating disorders such as anorexia and bulimia can be an attempt to change the body. For cisgender people, body changes are often motivated by the idea that weight loss will lead to increased self-confidence or provide control. In transgender clients, however, weight loss per se is not necessarily the goal. Instead, changing the body through weight loss (or gain) is a response to being born into what many of our clients call "the wrong body." (referencing an incongruence between gender identity and biological traits). While there is a perception that chronic binging or restricting will bring increased self-esteem, this is rarely the case.

What is it like to be in a body incongruent with gender identity? While gender identity is internal, the external body mediates how others see us. The lack of congruence between body, internal identity, and others' reactions leads to persistent negative feelings about self. Think back to Jared from Chapter 1. Jared's natural body type, slender and petite, did not match his internal male identity. Jared's eating disorder started as a way to "bulk up" and become more masculine. This is not always a fully conscious manifestation, and in Jared's case led to its own complications. While Jared felt more confident and masculine in the body that resulted from his binge eating, he also felt ashamed by his lack of control. When feeling pressured to cis-identify, Jared would eat very restrictively. This would again accentuate more feminine body traits. During a period of restrictive eating, Jared described this challenge: "I see myself in the mirror, a girl, with long hair and feminine clothing. And then I see *me*." The "me" he referenced was the male self and body he greatly desired. The roller coaster of binge/restrict continued, and Jared was ultimately hospitalized due to severe depression and a suicide attempt.

Such struggles are also complex in clients who are nonbinary. Consider 17-year-old Taylor.

Taylor identifies as pangender and prefers they/them pronouns. They explored numerous terms to describe their gender identity—gender fluid and gender expansive—before connecting with pangender as most descriptive of their experience. Taylor entered therapy for assistance navigating negative body image and binge/purge/restrict behaviors. Taylor felt pressured by peers at their former high school to connect with one of the binary genders and to look a certain way. Taylor's binge behaviors would increase when trying to present as masculine, and the purge/restrict behaviors would manifest when trying to present feminine. As they gained awareness of their gender identity outside the traditional male-female binary system, Taylor separated from their former high school environment. Taylor was able to create a new relationship to body and body image while decreasing dependence on eating-disorder behaviors to manipulate their body.

Attaining body congruence

Stories such as these highlight the need for clinicians to be more aware of clients' reasons for changing their bodies. Unlike others with eating disorders whose end goal is often to conform to the thin ideal, gender-expansive clients strive for congruence between body and gender. While social transition, affirming medical care, and corrective surgeries may be a healthier way to attain body congruence, clients may not take these steps. Instead, they may use eating-disorder symptoms to attain body congruence.

Common themes are:

- restrictive eating/excessive exercise to reduce curves and breasts and look more masculine ("boyish," flat, no curves, no hips)

- restriction as a way to change the body into a smaller, more feminine one (thin, "fragile," petite, small)

- restriction (limiting food intake, use of diet pills, and weight loss) as a way to stop the menstrual cycle

- restriction as a way to combat weight gain in transgender women on hormones

- laxative, diuretic abuse, and purging to counteract calorie consumption and reduce weight, leading to a reduction of body size and feminine characteristics

- binge eating to "bulk up" and appear more masculine (stocky, big, strong, manly)

- binge eating as way to hide the body and self

- injection of silicone use/abuse (non-medically supervised) to enhance breasts, buttocks, changing shape without changing weight

- non-prescription hormone use to achieve a more masculine or feminine appearance.

Joanie is 24 years old. Our initial contact was with Joanie's grandmother, who was concerned about Joanie's lack of post-college ambition and a recent weight gain. In our first session, Joanie shared that they (preferred pronoun) identified as nonbinary. Prior to college, they felt "awful" in their body. Now Joanie was more comfortable in their body, which they felt was more androgynous and congruent with their gender identity. Joanie was not binge eating but, instead, had made a conscious effort to make their body bigger through protein supplements and exercise. Joanie ultimately wished to have top surgery but did not want hormones. Joanie would not be diagnosed with either gender dysphoria or an eating disorder.

Like Joanie, not all clients have eating disorders, though it's helpful to routinely screen for them. Some questions to ask may include:

- What is your gender identity (male, female, agender, gender neutral, etc.)? Can you describe what this means?

- What do "male" bodies look like? "Female" bodies?

- Are there personality traits that you consider masculine and feminine? Food and eating behaviors?

- Are there things about your eating behaviors that you tend to keep a secret?

- Are there times when you eat more restrictively? Do you restrict certain food groups?

- Do you eat emotionally or binge eat? Are there ways you compensate when you have overeaten?

- What usually triggers restricting/binging/purging, and so on? Are there connections to your gender identity?

- What is the goal or function of your restricting/binging/purging, and so on?

Another strategy is a type of visual free association. We ask them to choose a word that best represents the goal of their eating disorder. For example, for restrictive eaters, the word may be "thin" or "fragile" and for binge eaters the word may be "comfort." They then write the word in the middle of a piece of paper, then write down other words that come to mind when they think about the word in the center. The word association for Juana, whom you met earlier in this chapter, is shown in Figure 8.2.

Figure 8.2: Juana's word associations

What do the word choices tell you about the function of Juana's disordered eating? Are the associations gendered in any way? What do they say about body image? This tool often provides a glimpse into the unique dynamics of the disordered eating among gender-expansive clients.

Reaction to stress and minority stress

Chapter 7 discussed numerous stressors in clients who are gender diverse. These stresses include experiences of mistreatment and discrimination at home and in school, as well as gender-based violence in the community. These experiences are pervasive and often repeated. While such stresses exist on a societal and interpersonal level, they also reside within the individual. Stigma includes the feelings people hold about themselves (such as internalized transphobia) or the beliefs they perceive others hold about them and that shape future behaviors. These stressors may be projected on the body, resulting in negative body image.

Studies have found that forms of stigma are highly prevalent among transgender people. Stigma has been linked to depression, anxiety, suicidality, and substance abuse (White Hughto, Reisner, & Pachankis, 2015; Randysner *et al.*, 2015; Sevelius, 2013).

Minority stress approaches view disordered eating behaviors as stress-induced responses to victimization, discrimination, and internalized stigma (Calzo *et al.*, 2017). Factors such as shame, concealing one's gender identity, and experiencing discrimination can lead to eating disorders. These stressors are projected on the body, increasing negative body image. In many cases, minority stress and trauma are directly connected to the body. Many of our clients describe being harassed because they are not "masculine" or "feminine" in their physical appearance or gender expression. Using an eating disorder to change the body may help them pass as their gender. It may even help them feel safer in their body.

Although minority stress approaches are on the mark when it comes to many kinds of mental health concerns, the complexity in clients with eating disorders makes it difficult to isolate this as the only factor. Minority stressors, in *combination* with the sense of body incongruence/gender dysphoria is what leads to disordered eating (see Figure 8.3). Treatment, then, addresses both factors (minority stress and body-image concerns) simultaneously.

Developed by Dalzell, Protos, & Hunt

Figure 8.3: Eating disorder influences

Consider the complexity of the following case.

Rickie is a 16-year-old client who identifies as a transgender male. Rickie's mother is not supportive of issues related to gender identity, and Rickie's father is more neutral. Rickie's mother has acknowledged that her concerns are fear-based. She "constantly obsesses" over whether Rickie will experience violence and bullying if Rickie is more open about his gender identity. Rickie's mother is critical of friends who are openly LGBT, stating that they are "influencing" Rickie. Recently, Rickie began eating more restrictively. Rickie said that this was a way to try to "make my body right" and to "get rid of curves." Rickie's mother became angrier at the weight loss, telling Rickie that he looked like "an ugly girl, not a boy." Rather than decreasing food restriction, Rickie now felt as if he was finally "on the right track." This idea became stronger as Rickie's dieting stopped menstruation. Treatment focused on the feelings Rickie had of being in the wrong body (one that menstruated), the lack of family support, comments about appearance, misgendering, and eating-disorder symptoms.

With Rickie, then, it was important to simultaneously address the minority stress (lack of family support, concealing identity), gender identity, and body dysphoria. Addressing one in the absence of the other factors would have been ineffective.

Response to gender identity/body incongruence

Another common connection between disordered eating and gender-identity concerns the confusion many people experience about gender identity. When people first begin to recognize that they may not identify as cisgender, it can be confusing. Think back to the exercise at the beginning of the chapter. You may have thought, "But I'm a woman—how can I see myself with a penis?" or "I'm a man—how can I have breasts?" You may have simply been confused by the entire exercise, or decided, "I'm not going there."

Our clients describe similar experiences that may begin with a "knowing but not knowing." Consider Cayden, whom we have referenced several times in this book. Cayden initially sought therapy for an eating disorder, but through our work together he later recognized his trans identity. Both of Cayden's parents routinely commented that there was "something else going on" besides the eating disorder. Similarly, Lisa, a 37-year-old client, struggled with anorexia since her teen years. "I knew something was not right with my body," she said. "I hated breasts and curves." When Lisa was able to get the anorexia under enough control to begin exploring identity, she initially identified as lesbian. The lack of acceptance she faced from her religiously conservative family led her to seek support within the queer community. As Lisa gained acceptance, she has since identified in a more fluid way. She has found comfort in the idea that she does not need to conform to a binary gender. She has also started to volunteer with LGBT youth as a mentor and has been open about her gender struggles. Her work with the youth organization and the ability to share her story have been an important part of her recovery.

Other clients describe having always recognized an expansive-gender identity but intentionally kept it secret. Secrecy can carry a significant emotional burden and also be a factor in eating disorders.

Affect modulation, distraction, and numbing

Eating disorders can also be a way of numbing the pain of secrets or of emotions connected to various stressors. Eating disorders can be used to numb powerful emotions. One of our clients, Nolan, was experiencing severe bullying in his high school. He describes his anorexia as a way to distract from these experiences and to numb emotions. Michelle, a woman in her 40s, describes similar functions for her bulimia. Michelle was involved in an intensely abusive relationship with her partner, Candice. Physically abusive, Candice would also belittle Michelle's physical appearance. Candice would also routinely threaten to leave Michelle for a "real woman." Michelle binged to numb her feelings, while purging allowed her to compensate for the calories she consumed. Michelle's binging continued until she was able to leave the relationship. Healthy coping skills can help clients manage feelings and distract them from emotional pain.

Conforming to body image ideals

Sociocultural approaches view disordered eating as rooted in minority-specific norms concerning ideal appearance or the importance of appearance and physical attributes (Calzo *et al.*, 2017). There have been a number of studies that suggest that disordered eating is more prevalent in LGBT-identified people (especially gay men and black and Latino people). There are varying risk factors, including discrimination and fear of rejection, internalized negative messages and beliefs about oneself due to expansive gender expressions, or transgender identity.

While much is known about body image ideals of LGBT populations, research about gender-expansive people as a whole is in its infancy. One study aptly titled "I have to constantly prove to myself, to people, that I fit the bill" (Gordon *et al.*, 2016) mirrors many of the things we see with our clients. Though societal norms to conform to ideals of masculinity and femininity affect many of our clients, trans people are often even more highly impacted. Such ideals include bodies that are classically masculine or feminine.

Pressures to pass, then, may be coupled with experiences communicating that appearance or behavior is not "masculine" or "feminine" enough. Michelle, whom you just met, was less traumatized by her partner's physical abuse than by the disparagement of her appearance and femininity. Other have been publicly shamed for not passing, for example while using public bathrooms. Adrian, a trans male client, had been on testosterone for more than a year and was awaiting top surgery, which was postponed due to financial constraints. As a large-breasted person, Adrian found binding physically uncomfortable. He was chastised by several men when using a public restroom and was repeatedly asked what gender he was. This precipitated a severe depression and feelings of hopelessness that things would not change after surgery. When Adrian did have surgery, his self-esteem and body image improved dramatically. He was subsequently able to use the men's restroom without fear.

The concerns discussed in this chapter affect our clients. Maintaining awareness of the functions of eating disorders and the interconnections to gender identity and minority stress are essential. We will talk more about the treatment of body image and eating disorders in the next chapter.

FOR FURTHER EXPLORATION

- If you have not already done so, try out the body-image visualization at the beginning of the chapter. Consciously imagine your body changing to incorporate gendered features of the sex you were not assigned at birth (i.e., if you are female, imagine yourself as a male). Take some time to write about your reactions.

- On a piece of paper, write the words "My Body" in the center of the page. Spend about ten minutes associating to the words, writing down what comes to mind. What did you notice? Do any of the words reflect a desire to be larger or smaller? Are there any gendered words? Judgmental words?

- Where are you on the body image continuum? Is this a comfortable place? Take a moment to define the ideas of "body acceptance" and "body ownership." What behaviors do you already engage in that reflect body acceptance? Body ownership? How can you use your experiences with this exercise to support your clients better?

Chapter 9

Treating Eating Disorders, Gender Dysphoria, and Minority Stress

In the previous chapter, you met Juana, a 35-year-old Latina transgender client who once struggled with restrictive and binge eating. She no longer uses these symptoms as a way to cope with the stresses associated with gender identity. Working with Juana and other clients with gender dysphoria has taught us a lot about the recovery process. While treatment can be similar to cisgender clients, there are important differences.

When we first met Juana, she was in her late 20s and had not yet come out as trans. At that time, she identified as a bisexual cisgender man. Juana's weight was well below what was acceptable, given her taller, ectomorphic body frame. Juana's partner, Sam, who was well into his 40s, came with her to her first appointment. Sam was encouraging but paternal. Juana had been recently hospitalized but was discharged without a significant weight gain. Since discharge, Juana was eating only one small meal per day, limiting fluid intake, and had also been using ephedrine-based diet pills.

The couple described numerous stressors: a lack of acceptance from Juana's traditional Catholic family (who had expected their son to be "macho," straight and successful) and Juana's long-standing anorexia. Juana had also recently left the Coast Guard following a deployment to remediate an oil spill in the Gulf of Mexico. The aftermath left Juana, an avid animal lover, traumatized. She was having frequent nightmares and intrusive thoughts. Juana had been bullied (homophobic and anti-Latino slurs) while in the service. She closed up when probed about this. Juana was experiencing PTSD symptoms. The racism and homophobia likely contributed to this.

Juana did not disclose struggles with gender identity, and the initial treatment plan involved working through minority stressors, resolving her PTSD, and stabilizing her weight. Supporting her in reducing her gender dysphoria was added later.

While Juana's story may seem complicated, it reflects the varied experiences of many of our clients.

Treatment model

Treatment with clients this complex involves a number of inter-connected components. Our paradigm draws on the theoretical lens of intersectionality, looking at how social identities such as race, class, sexuality, and gender interact with pre-existing traumas, mood disorders, and gender dysphoria to increase a client risk's of eating disorders and negative body image. Using this lens, we also look at those areas that enable recovery.

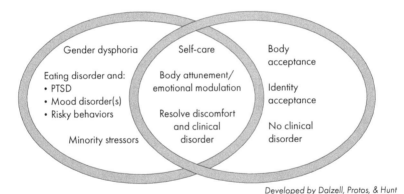

Developed by Dalzell, Protos, & Hunt

Figure 9.1: Model for client with eating disorder and gender identity concerns

The left side of Figure 9.1 illustrates the many areas that our clients struggle with. Clients typically have a combination of gender dysphoria, eating disorders (or body image concerns), and minority stressors. Many of our clients also have other mood symptoms, such as anxiety or panic, and engage in risky behaviors. These behaviors may be connected to the eating disorder (such as diuretic abuse or stimulant abuse) or separate from it (such as heavy alcohol use or deliberate self-harm).

The right side of the model shows a person with body/identity acceptance and no clinical disorders. This is a type of "clinical unicorn" in our practice, although it is the goal. In addition, therapy alone may be insufficient to allow clients to fully accept their bodies and identities. This may require medical steps, such as hormone therapies or surgeries.

The intersection of the two sides—and the work of therapy—is a combination of self-care, body attunement, and emotional modulation. These factors support clients in decreasing or resolving symptoms of eating disorders. When clients begin to value themselves and to care for themselves differently, they are more able to embrace their identities (whether gender-based, racial, sexual, etc.) We also focus on accompanying disorders, such as PTSD. For example, Juana benefitted from eye movement desensitization and reprocessing (EMDR), which helped with PTSD symptoms connected with the acute trauma of the oil spill.

Conducting a needs assessment

The first step in our treatment approach is a solid needs assessment, looking at major components associated with gender identity, eating disorders, other symptoms, and minority stressors.

The needs assessment looks at various factors that contribute to a client's eating disorder. Clinicians can consider any of the topics listed in bold type in Table 9.1 when looking at a client's history and symptom presentation. For example, what does your client tell you about gender identity? Does the client identify as trans, fluid? Is this identification positive or negative?

The needs assessment is a dynamic tool and can be updated as needed. Juana's needs assessment is given in Table 9.1.

Table 9.1: Juana's needs assessment*

Components associated with gender dysphoria	
Gender identity	Trans identity: desire to be a woman; hopelessness
Openness vs. secrecy	Fear of disclosure, fears that others will reject efforts to transition
Support system vs. lack of support system	No current support system to allow for exploration of gender and body congruence

Eating disorder, risky behaviors, PTSD, other	
Eating disorder diagnosis	Long-standing struggles with disordered eating, belief that it could decrease masculine traits; chronic dieting; binge eating alternates; over-control by partner
Body image	Negative view of body size and shape (preference to be "slight," "dainty"), dislike of height and broad frame, desire to change body/transition (hormones, surgery, etc.), lack of overall self-care
Risky behaviors connected to disordered eating	One meal daily, limiting fluid intake, excessive exercise, ephedrine-based diet pills
Post-traumatic stress disorder	PTSD symptoms connected to incidences of bullying and acute PTSD as a result of recent work-based trauma (oil spill), poor sleep/nightmares, intrusive memories
Other (e.g., other negative coping skills or diagnoses)	N/A
Minority stressors (list all stressors)	
Homophobia/ transphobia	Comments from others, including family, about "lifestyle choices," bullying from co-workers, fears about transitioning
Family rejection	Rejection from conservative family
Racism	Slurs about Latino origins

* Following gender identity disclosure

Juana's needs assessment illustrates the many areas that may require support to reach our goals of increasing self-care and body attunement and resolving symptoms. It provides a road map of how to proceed.

Self-care, body attunement

Self-care refers to the act of clients taking an active role in protecting their well-being and happiness, especially during periods of stress. Self-care activities may include basics, such as getting enough sleep or showering daily. They may include activities that involve self-care and are also used as coping strategies, such as bubble baths or meditation. Many clients, especially those with eating disorders, lack the motivation to care for themselves. This makes sense when you consider that proper nourishment is a form of self-care.

Many gender-expansive clients have difficulties with self-care. This often reflects body dysphoria and discomfort. Rowan, a ten-year-old trans female client, refused to bathe or shower because she hated seeing male body parts. This did not get better until much later when Rowan started hormones and could see physical changes.

Body attunement is a closely connected idea. This is the ability to care for oneself appropriately when cued by the body. Thus, body attunement is the ability to listen to body cues and respond to these cues. Simple examples are eating when hungry and sleeping when tired.

People with disordered eating patterns ignore body signals. For instance, people with binge eating ignore satiety signals, prompting them to overeat. They may also override prompts that indicate fatigue, binging in response to being tired. People with anorexia ignore hunger, as do chronic dieters.

Body attunement plays a role in regulating emotions. Rowan had difficulty with body attunement and did not listen to her body when she was tired and needed to take breaks. Rowan's inability to sense her internal states of tiredness or feeling overwhelmed led to frequent meltdowns.

Rowan also had issues with food texture and was a classically picky eater. Her emotional lapses resulted in even pickier and more restrictive food intake. These patterns are common in adult clients, who may continue working to the point of exhaustion (and binge to "energize").

Emotional regulation involves effective communication between body, mind, and feelings. When people are under stress, they need to be able to accurately identify and evaluate physiological signals and choose appropriate regulation strategies that reduce emotional responses (Price & Hooven, 2018).

Putting it all together

All of these things work in tandem. Let's return to Juana, whose needs assessment you saw earlier in this chapter.

Early in treatment, Juana had not disclosed that she was trans, but did describe body image and eating concerns. Juana was disconnected from her body and hated it passionately. She described it as "too large," "beefy," and "clumsy." Restricting food intake allowed Juana to attain a "smaller," more "fragile" body. Though acutely aware of her hunger signals, Juana ate one small meal a day. Despite her minimal food and fluid intake, Juana worked out for several hours a day. These symptoms were worsening with each passing day. Juana and Sam were opposed to the idea of re-hospitalization. Her physician agreed to monitor her weight and medical stability.

We further explored Juana's restricting by using a word-association exercise, as shown in Figure 8.2. In this exercise, Juana associated to the keyword "thin." Some of the words Juana selected included "delicate," "slight," and "dainty." When probed about gender identity and the feminine nature of these words, Juana disclosed a secret: she fantasized about being a small, fine-featured woman. "It's what I've always dreamed about," she said "but I've tried so hard to just be a man." Juana cried for the remainder of the session.

After disclosing her identity, Juana was relieved but also felt a hopelessness that she could ever transition. She did not believe that her family could accept her as a woman and feared that Sam would leave her. Juana was doubtful that she could ever feel comfortable in her body. We spent many sessions validating the difficulty of these feelings and gently challenging the all-or-nothing nature of the negative beliefs.

A turning point occurred when Juana involved Sam in the discussion. Sam was initially surprised about Juana's gender identity and was uncertain about what this would mean to the relationship. Despite this, he reiterated that he loved Juana and would support her.

We began to talk about the importance of a healthy body as a prerequisite to transition. Juana started to make changes. This included increasing body connection, using grounding and guided meditation. Juana discontinued the diet pills and added water to her meals. Juana also kept a hunger log, which helped her to notice how hungry she was. A dietician joined Juana's treatment team, something Juana had been opposed to in the past.

Juana slowly began to eat more frequently and take in more at each meal. Juana was also able to limit time at the gym, and to rest when she was tired. When Juana came down with a bad cold that zapped her strength, she skipped exercise that day. This was a huge victory for her as she'd never been able to take a day off from exercising. She celebrated this achievement.

Sam continued to be supportive, providing Juana with reassurance about her changing body.

Other components of self-care/pleasure in the body

When clients successfully manage self-care and response to body cues, it's time to up the ante. The next phase involves promoting pleasurable body-related activities. This can feel scary or overwhelming in the initial phases of treatment, but can make the difference in moving toward body acceptance. While there are many metaphors to explain this, thinking about a car can be helpful. If you have a car that you don't like or only tolerate, you will likely do only the basics to care for it. But if you really love your car, you will be sure it stays clean, perhaps pay for detailing, and maintain it well. Clients can learn to accept—and to love—their bodies.

We introduce the idea of body pleasure through a series of questions, beginning with basic questions such as, "How do you take care of your body?" ("I take a shower every day.") Clients can be less comfortable with questions, such as, "How do you take pleasure in your body?" It takes time to move from body disconnection to body connection and nurturance. The eventual goal is to incorporate activities which focus on feeling good in the body.

Other questions to ask about body pleasure are presented on in the box that follows.

Questions to promote awareness of body pleasure

- How do you take care of your body?

- How do you take pleasure in your body?

- When does your body feel good? Not so good?

- When is the best you have felt physically? What activities are most pleasurable?

- How do you know when know when something is wrong with your body?

- What foods do you enjoy eating? What makes these enjoyable?

- Do you enjoy masturbation? Sex? What is enjoyable about these activities? What could make it feel even better?

- What is your favorite season? What sensory experiences (sight, sounds, smells, tastes, movement) add to the enjoyment?

- How do you prefer to move in your body? What do you notice during healthy movement? Afterwards? Can you stay in your body?

- What are your favorite scents?

- How can you make your physical environment more beautiful? What does your body notice about the beauty?

- What is your relationship to alcohol, drugs, cigarettes, and other substances?

This is also a good time to introduce concepts such as mindfulness and body-awareness practices. Jon Kabat-Zinn, one of the earliest writers about mindfulness, says mindfulness means paying attention in a particular way: on purpose, in the present moment, and non-judgmentally. It can involve awareness of the sensory experiences of something, such as really noticing a shower, a walk in the park, or a delicious meal. Clients who are more mindful allow themselves to fully experience pleasure ("I take a mindful shower every day, noticing the feel of the water on my body and the pleasure of standing under the warm spray").

The practices contained in the following box can also be helpful.

Ways to build body attunement and pleasure

- Yoga/breathing

- Music

- Meditation

- Mindful walks, baths, showers, eating

- Journaling

- Grounding and body scans

- Adding in complementary practices, such as Randi ki or massage

- Aromatherapy

- Gentle movement (walks, stretching).

Juana was initially hesitant to experience any pleasure in her body. As she began to eat more consistently, and she worked on mindfulness, she was open to the idea of a mindful walk. She felt more relaxed and engaged as she noticed her surroundings fully, and enjoyed the tactile pleasure associated with walking. Juana started in a trauma-informed yoga class. At first this was a stretch, as she was almost too aware of her body and its incongruencies. As Juana began hormone treatment and saw more feminization, she felt more comfortable in the yoga class.

Juana and Sam's sex life also improved, and she credited this with being more aware of self-care and body pleasure. This helped the overall relationship. Sam no longer felt he had to be a caretaker to Juana, and their relationship equalized. The couple began to act more like partners than father/daughter.

Identifying emotions

Body attunement is essential in identifying and managing emotions. While some clients are acutely aware of their own—and others'—emotions, other clients are not. Therapy can promote and increase awareness of emotions and how emotions manifest in the body. When clients talk about something that makes them angry or sad, we ask what they notice in their bodies and where they notice these sensations. For example, when Juana described a situation in which she ran into a cousin who pretended not to know her, she was angry. While processing the situation, Juana was able to place the anger in her jaw, neck, and hands. The anger felt "intense, sharp, tense, and knotted." Eventually, Juana was able to notice those feelings and tolerate them for long time frames; when she needed to, she would walk or do some deep breathing.

Working on minority stress, gender dysphoria, and body image
Trans-affirmative cognitive behavioral therapy (TA-CBT)

The preparatory steps just discussed provide a solid foundation from which to work on gender dysphoria and minority stress. Our world is often invalidating of diverse identities and body expressions. Clients need tools to address the reality of such invalidating experiences.

Cognitive-behavioral approaches are particularly well suited to working on minority stressors. Trans-affirmative cognitive behavioral therapy (TA-CBT) (Austin & Craig, 2015; Austin, Craig, & D'Souza 2017; Austin, Craig, & Alessi, 2017) is a short-term therapeutic approach that teaches strategies to address minority stressors. TA-CBT adapts traditional CBT approaches to serve the needs of transgender and gender-expansive clients. This is a best practice approach.

Like traditional CBT approaches, the heart of TA-CBT involves the idea that thoughts affect emotions and behaviors. Clients learn to replace maladaptive coping behaviors, such as eating-disorder symptoms, with more effective coping skills. TA-CBT also supports clients in exploring and understanding how anti-LGBT attitudes and behaviors influence stress. While TA-CBT validates and affirms that trans and gender-expansive people often have difficult life experiences, it teaches them to challenge negative thinking and internalized transphobia. This approach also focuses on developing safe, supportive, and identity-affirming social networks.

We adapt TA-CBT to meet the needs of our clients, and these are some of our treatment goals:

- Normalize mental health consequences of minority stress and its connection to eating disorders.

- Support client's realities that their current body does not conform with internal gender identity or body ideals.

- Validate feelings surrounding body incongruence.

- Challenge dysfunctional coping skills (such as restricting, binging, or purging).

- Support effective, safe practices for changing the body (clothing and hair, hormones, surgical interventions).

- Facilitate supportive relationships (LGBT social groups, LGBT-friendly eating-disorder groups) that foster therapeutic goals.

- Support assertive behaviors.

Some examples of how to respond to difficult scenarios are show in Table 9.2.

Table 9.2: Responses to difficult scenarios using TA-CBT approaches

Situation	Sample response
Support the client's reality that their current body does not conform with their internal gender identity or body ideals	Acknowledge and validate feelings: "What you are seeing in the mirror *is* different from what you would ideally like to see. Are there more adaptive ways to cope than restricting?"
Validate feelings surrounding body incongruence	Acknowledge and validate feelings: "It is true that most women do not need to shave. That does not feel good."
Challenge dysfunctional coping skills (such as restricting, binging, or purging)	Recognize emotional consequences of situation: "It must have been hard that the server commented on your appetite, and I can see why you coped by restricting. Was there another way you could have responded?"
Support effective, safe practices for changing the body	Focus on resilience: "You are doing what you can and it's hard to wait. Hormones take time to work in the way you are seeking."
Facilitate supportive relationships and decrease avoidance behaviors	Acknowledge feelings while promoting positive behaviors: "It is hard to go into a context where you are unsure about acceptance. I've had other trans clients attend this meeting and they have had great experiences."
Acknowledge transphobic policies	Acknowledge transphobic policies: "That situation did feel very isolating. Are you handling it in the most effective way you can?"
Support assertive behaviors	Acknowledge transphobic policies and take assertive action: "It is frustrating that that program does not take trans men. Perhaps you could call your insurance company to seek support from a program that does."

Creating a body image hope box

Another useful tool that Austin and Craig (2015) recommend is a hope box. While traditionally, people create hope boxes to help foster hope when they have suicidal thoughts, our adaptation fosters a more positive body image.

To create a body image hope box, have the client decorate a box large enough to hold several of the objects below. They can then decorate the box in any creative way that they prefer. The box can hold:

- personalized objects or symbols that reflect future goals (e.g., a bracelet that says "Dream")

- role models (i.e., celebrities who have transitioned, activists) before and after

- sources of support and interpersonal connection

- a list of future goals and ideas

- a love letter to yourself or your body

- Encouraging letters from friends

- photos of places that are safe or have felt joyful

- body-positive song lyrics

- inspirational quotes about body image

- self/body affirmations ("I am a work in progress"; "I am willing to embrace the parts of me that need it the most"; "I am learning to be at peace with who I am now, and I'm excited about who I can be")

- poems (such as by trans poets Andrea Gibson, Trace Peterson).

These tools can be helpful in working on minority stress and body image. Additionally, clients may need support in managing other clinical concerns, including PTSD.

Other clinical concerns, including PTSD

Clients like Juana often come to therapy requiring specific interventions for trauma. Trauma-informed therapies can support resolution of PTSD. There are many such therapies: EMDR, prolonged exposure, cognitive processing therapy, narrative therapy, to name a few.

Trauma-informed therapies focus on the memory of the traumatic event and its meaning. For example, while experiences such as identity-based bullying are distressing, people may internalize them in different ways. Some, for example, may be left with a feeling of not being safe ("I'm in danger"). Others may internalize them as a measure of self-worth ("I am disgusting"), or as a lack of control ("I am powerless"). They may also blame themselves for the trauma—something that is particularly common in cases of internalized homophobia ("It's all my fault").

As Juana began to gain weight, the breadth of the traumas began to emerge. These included rejection by her father, who could not tolerate a sensitive/less traditionally masculine son, and ridicule from siblings about Juana's more effeminate presentation. These childhood traumas were connected to Juana's emerging identity as a trans woman. A narrative approach, allowed Juana to understand that her gender identity aligned with her values (especially the compassion she felt towards others and animals). Juana began to question some of the long-standing cognitions she had about herself and her worth, including the belief that she was somehow "damaged." She also began to see that many of the abuse experiences in the service were extensions of the childhood bullying, and that she had essentially traded one abusive and rejecting family for another. While these recognitions were hard, Juana found the insight helpful.

Even after processing these early traumas, Juana continued to have PTSD symptoms. With the vivid visual nature of her re-experiencing symptoms, EMDR was an effective approach that helped to clear the remaining negative cognitions associated with the oil spill. These included, "I could have done more," and "I deserve to be miserable." Juana was able to understand that she had done all she could to help remediate the spill, and that she did not need to be punished for not having done more.

Following EMDR, Juana also began to understand and more fully accept that the years of hiding and trying to fit in as a man were part of the problem. She came out more widely, and while her father continued to be rejecting, she has seen a softening in her mother's attitude. Juana has felt more hopeful that her mother may be able to one day accept her as a daughter. Sam has remained a loving support following Juana's transition.

FOR FURTHER EXPLORATION

- Think about a client that you have seen in your practice. Do a needs assessment, breaking down client concerns into the areas of gender dysphoria, clinical concerns, and minority stressors. What areas would be helpful to address in treatment?

- Think about your own life. Can you improve your self-care? Body attunement? Eat more intuitively? What are some proactive steps you could take to accomplish these goals?

- Practice mindfulness: after brushing your teeth and preparing for your day, take a mindful shower. Be aware of the sound of the water, the feeling of it on your face, its temperature, and your sense of groundedness as you stand there. Also notice the taste of the toothpaste in your mouth, the smell of the soap. Write about this experience.

- Create your own body image hope box. What would you include in the box and why?

Chapter 10

Gender Affirmation, Body Changes, and their Effects (Transitioning)

"How does it feel? It's like my body knows that it has the right chemicals flowing through it. I know it doesn't work that way, but the moment I took the first dose of hormones I felt…right. More 'right' in my body than I can ever remember feeling. I'm afraid something will change and this feeling will go away, and then I remember that nothing can take this away from me now." (Erik, a 17-year-old gender-nonbinary client after the first few days on hormones)

"I will never forget that moment. I was on the exam table with my father beside me. The doctor asked, 'Are you ready?' I replied, 'So ready!' The doctor took off the surgical compression tape around my chest. He handed me a mirror. I saw my chest—a male chest—for the very first time. I was still swollen from the surgery, but I could see myself clearly for the first time in this body. In my body. There were no words at that moment. I saw my father crying and felt supported. After so many years of planning for this moment, it was here. I felt at peace." (Cayden, a 25-year-old transmasculine client after top surgery)

What does the term "transition" mean to you? Have you experienced any transitions in your life? Perhaps you are thinking about the transition to adulthood that occurs in late adolescence. Perhaps you are thinking about other life transitions, such as giving birth, children leaving for college, retiring after a busy career. Call to mind one transition that resonates with you. What did you feel during this time? Were you excited? Scared? Hesitant? A mix of emotions?

In the gender-expansive community, *transition* refers to the process people go through to align their internal gender identity with their external physical appearance. While not all gender-expansive people transition, many take these steps. Transitioning can help to address gender and body dysphoria, increase self-esteem and body confidence, and support recovery from eating disorders.

There are three primary types of transition: social transition (using a different name, dressing in a way more congruent with gender), legal transition (legally changing name or gender marker), and medical transition (hormones or surgery to alter the body). People may choose to transition any, all or none of these ways.

This chapter will discuss transition at all ages, youth through adult, and will include research findings about how transition affects mental health outcomes. We will also look at assessment issues and informed consent.

Types of gender transition

Pat (a trans male) is excited. At the age of 52, he has decided to transition to male. Pat's wide smile belies the past difficulties he's had. Pat has known that he identifies as a man for some time, but had always been afraid to take steps to transition. His divorce is now final and his son has completed college. His chronic depression, binge eating, and body hatred seem to have receded with the decision to transition. Pat has thought through the pros and cons of hormones and top surgery and has scheduled an appointment with the trans health center. As we discuss the idea of social transition, Pat is intrigued by the idea that his transition can begin before surgery. He is enthusiastic to try binding and to dress more in a more masculine manner.

Had you met Pat at an earlier stage in his journey, such as when he needed to hide his gender identity, this animated and cheerful man would likely have acted quite differently. He may have been depressed, anxious, or hated his body.

Clients come to therapy at many stages of transition. Some have not yet recognized or accepted that their gender identity does not match their assigned sex. Others, like Pat, have contemplated their gender for some time and want to proceed with some form of transition. Exploring transition is often a key part of therapy.

For clients with co-occurring eating disorders, taking concrete measures to affirm gender identity through transition may decrease restrictive eating, binging, or purging. Many people describe relief from various mental health challenges as they express their gender identity in an outward way.

Social transition

Social transition (also called social affirmation) is the process of making others aware of one's gender by expressing gender in a way that is congruent with internal gender identity. Social affirmation can include choosing a new name and using pronouns more in line with identity or changing physical appearance (clothing choices, hairstyle, binding/packing). Clients may go through several phases of social transition, perhaps beginning by asking family members or friends to use different pronouns, then selecting a name that feels right, and experimenting with hairstyles or dressing more androgynously or in a more masculine or feminine way.

Terry is a teen client who struggles with restrictive eating. Terry continues to use she/her pronouns. She is unsure whether she is transgender but feels that her identity may be nonbinary. Terry has a short haircut and dresses androgynously, wearing T-shirts bearing band logos/slogans and boys' jeans. One of the things that has significantly helped with Terry's restrictive eating has been experimenting with a binder. "I feel much more comfortable now," Terry says. "I know it sounds weird, but when I ate I was scared my chest would get bigger. Now I see a visibly smaller chest and am less afraid."

Albert, whom you met in Chapter 7, knew he wanted the name Albert from the moment he connected with being a trans man. Albert's birth name was Alice. He comes from a religious family who are not supportive of trans people. Albert has asked them to call him "Al" as a compromise. When family members call him Alice, he is hurt and will not respond to them. Their use of his "dead name" has been a trigger for Albert's depression and binge eating. At other times, his chosen name feels like a comfort and helps with his long-standing body dissatisfaction.

Lindsey, a transfeminine client in her late 20s, is uncomfortable presenting as female in most social settings. She fears derogatory remarks from others. In safe spaces, Lindsey wears traditionally feminine clothes and makeup. She styles her hair with headbands and hair clips. Lindsey watches cisgender women and tries to emulate their posture, gait, and mannerisms. While Lindsey struggles with body image and restrictive eating to appear smaller and more feminine, she is more comfortable in her body when she dresses in a feminine way. She hopes to transition medically soon, and is optimistic that the resulting physical changes will decrease the pressure she feels to control her weight.

How can we, as therapists, help our clients with social transition? One of the most important things is to meet clients where they are in this process. If they are not yet ready for social transition, that's OK. If they are, we can provide a safe space to experiment with gender identity. Would clients feel safe presenting as their preferred gender in your office? If not, how could you increase their sense of safety? One of our therapists has a client who wanted to wear a dress to sessions but was fearful of walking into the waiting room in a dress. The therapist suggested that her client change clothes in the staff bathroom. This allowed her client to be more comfortable during their session and to process how she felt.

Therapy can help to bridge social transition. Clients often need a place to discuss how choices affect them. What pronouns do they prefer? What name? How did it feel to wear a binder for the first time? To pack? Are they afraid to shop in the male or female section of a department store? Is online shopping a better choice? Often, clients need a place to talk through these choices and to express their fears, hopes, and dreams.

Body changes and medical transition

Many clients find that social transition, while helpful, is not enough. They continue to experience body dissatisfaction, gender dysphoria, or eating disorders. These clients may choose to explore medical interventions, including hormones and surgical procedures.

Erik and Cayden, who were quoted in the opening passage of this chapter, both had eating disorders. Medical intervention—hormones in Erik's case and hormones and surgery in Cayden's—helped to improve body image and decrease the symptoms of their eating disorders. In thinking back to these opening quotes, what emotions do you identify in their experiences? Do you have clients who have expressed similar emotions about physical steps in transition? For Erik and Cayden, changing the body through these medical interventions created a more positive body image.

The box below outlines a number of options for medical transition.

Medical transition

Hormone therapy and suppression:

- Puberty blockers

- Masculinizing hormones

- Feminizing hormones.

Gender confirmation surgeries:

- Transfeminine top surgery

- Transfeminine bottom surgery

- Facial feminization surgery

- Transmasculine top surgery

- Transmasculine bottom surgery

- Facial masculinization surgery.

Other methods:

- Laser hair removal

- Voice training.

While medical intervention is possible at any age, it can be especially helpful for clients who have not yet hit puberty. Puberty blockers, for example, can pause the development of secondary sex characteristics. This allows gender-creative children more time to explore their gender identity. If the client decides to transition later on, the physical impact is easier to manage. If the client decides not to transition, the original puberty process will continue once the blockers are stopped.

Elijah, an assigned female at birth, began to express to his parents that he felt like a boy when he was six. His family supported him, and he socially transitioned choosing the name "Elijah" and dressing in boy's clothing. While this helped, Elijah struggled at this young age with body image and highly selective eating (avoidant restrictive food intake disorder). As he approached puberty, Elijah began to obsess about the physical changes that he knew were coming. When he began to develop breast buds, Elijah became suicidal. The family consulted with a pediatric specialist, who prescribed puberty blockers. The breast buds disappeared and his mood brightened. The family is discussing timing and next steps, and are leaning towards masculinizing hormones.

Isabel's experience with hormones is another example of the positive impact of medical intervention. She found feminizing hormones "life changing." Isabel struggled with severe depression and suicidal thoughts for years, before she came out as transgender at the age of 25. Isabel felt disconnected from herself and everyone around her, trapped in an incongruent body. Supportive family and friends encouraged her to try hormones, which helped. Isabel is also using laser hair removal to assist with dysphoria associated with unwanted body hair. While physically painful, it is less emotionally painful than the dysphoria associated with shaving. As Isabel has transitioned, she is less depressed and is eating more consistently. She is also more connected to others.

At the beginning of the chapter, we witnessed Cayden's experience with gender confirmation surgery. Breasts were a particular area of body discomfort, but financial realities and an active eating disorder delayed the surgery. When Cayden realized he had to be physically nourished and emotionally ready for surgery, he began to make progress in his eating disorder. Following surgery, Cayden's body image has improved significantly.

Like Cayden, many clients struggle with the financial aspect of medical interventions. While some insurance carriers offer support for gender-confirmation surgeries and transgender healthcare, exclusions can limit access to care. Some medical providers and surgeons who specialize in trans health either do not accept insurance or are self-pay only. For some patients, then, the financial burden is too great and is a barrier to transition.

People who go through medical transition generally need to be at least 18 years old or have the approval of legal guardians. While some families may be reluctant to consider medical interventions, they are preferable to unhealthy measures used attain a more identity-congruent body. Family members need a place to process their reactions to these options. They may also have medical questions, and resources that can answer these questions are invaluable. It is also helpful for adolescents to understand their families' reservations. Honor each person's experience.

Legal affirmation

Jamison is a 22-year-old trans male. He has recently gone through social and medical transition (hormones, top surgery) but has not been able to legally transition because of finances. In the state where he lives, legal transition (see below) will cost between $600 and $1000. He recently went to an eye doctor's appointment, and his insurance card was in his legal name (which is markedly female). He was uncomfortable being called his old name by staff. Jamison left the appointment and binged for the first time in a year. Fortunately, he realized that this was a slippery slope and got back on track. Jamison vowed to have his name legally changed as soon as he could.

Legal transition is the process of officially changing one's name and/or gender markers (indications of male and female) on legal documents, including transcripts, driver's license, passport (see the box below). While these changes may not have as direct an impact on body image as other aspects of transition, they play an important part in a client's ability to navigate diverse spaces. In many cases, documents that list one's dead name immediately out the person as gender expansive.

Requirements for legal name and/or gender-marker change vary from state to state. Some states still require surgery prior to gender-marker changes, but this is being relaxed in many places.

Items associated with name change

- Birth certificate

- Passport

- Driver's license

- Social Security card

- Transcripts and school records

- Professional licenses

- Bank statements

- Car registration

- Human resource documents

- Deeds to real estate.

Changing one's name is a powerful part of transition and identity acceptance. Many of our younger clients change their legal documents before graduating from high school. This allows for a smoother entrance to college or professional schools without their identifying documents outing their transgender or gender-expansive status.

To Maeve, a transfeminine, first-year college student, documentation matching her gender identity was equivalent to freedom. Throughout high school, the first day of class was anxiety-provoking: *Which name will they use? Did the instructor see my email asking for them to use my preferred name?* After finalizing her legal name change, her anxieties disappeared. She no longer feared being misgendered and no longer needed to binge or purge to manage anxiety.

Many universities also have housing options based on legal gender. While her campus had an option for gender-neutral housing, Maeve was grateful for the opportunity to choose between an all-girls' dormitory or the gender-neutral floor.

Our role as therapist–advocate is to help clients to understand their options and to connect them with resources to help them navigate this system. Create a document outlining the steps for legal name change. If possible, be ready with names and telephone numbers of trans-affirmative attorneys whom you know that clients can reliably access for support. Perhaps you know of a local agency with a free legal clinic or of legal advocates knowledgeable in this area.

Improvements in body image

How does transition affect body image? This is an important question, and research is beginning to look at this question. Observationally, all types of transition seem to promote positive change in body image and a reduction in eating-disorder symptoms. Most of the studies to date look at the effects of surgeries on body image. What we see clinically is also borne out in the research.

Dutch researchers van de Grift, Kreukels, and colleagues (2016b) looked at body image in trans men, specifically how mastectomy affects body satisfaction and attitude, appearance schemas, quality of life, and self-esteem. Before surgery, trans men were much less satisfied with their appearance and had poorer body image than cisgender men and women. After mastectomy, their body satisfaction improved. Respondents reported decreased dysphoria and improved self-worth. Similarly, El-Hadi, Stone, and Temple-Oberle (2018) studied 32 transgender individuals who medically transitioned. The researchers found that surgical transition was important to the quality of life for 91 percent of participants, and 100 percent were happy with their decision to undergo surgery. Their satisfaction may stem from their ability to pass as the gender they identify as.

Informed consent vs. gatekeeping: advocating for our clients

A common treatment request is for "letters of support" for hormones and surgery. Currently, many physicians and most insurance companies require that people seeking medical transition provide one or more letters from mental health providers which document that medical intervention is needed to alleviate gender dysphoria. Letters of support also indicate that people understand the risks and benefits of surgery. In other words, part of the clinical role is to assess informed consent.

Most clinicians are familiar with this concept. The American Medical Association defines informed consent as "the ethical and legal basis for most patient care decisions" (Cavanaugh, Hopwood, & Lambert, 2016). The informed-consent process includes helping clients understand potential risks and benefits of a given treatment. Informed consent is grounded in the client's capacity to weigh options. A key concept related to consent is self-determination—client autonomy over decisions. For gender-expansive clients, such informed consent includes the idea of body autonomy—the right to make decisions about medical aspects of transition.

The WPATH *Standards of Care*

The World Professional Association for Transgender Health (WPATH) has released a comprehensive set of guidelines, the WPATH *Standards of Care* (*SOC*) (Coleman *et al.*, 2012), which details best practices in transgender healthcare. While the WPATH *Standards of Care* were groundbreaking in outlining health considerations, they have come under fire in the transgender and gender-expansive community. The controversy focuses on the suggestion that clients need letters of support from mental health providers before starting hormones and/ or surgical procedures. People who advocate for a purely "informed-consent" standard seem to suggest that the desire to start surgery or take hormones is all that is needed.

Do these letters put clinicians in a gatekeeping role? Or are they another clinical support, or way of advocating for the client?

In thinking about these questions, let's look at the suggested format of support letters:

1. Statement of how long the clinician has known the client and a brief history of gender identity.

2. How the client has socially transitioned (if applicable).

3. A statement that the client has gender dysphoria that results in significant distress.

4. Medical and surgical history.

5. Mental health history, substance screening.

6. An assessment of informed consent.

7. A statement that the clinician supports the surgery.

While letters of support are required in many cases, many gender-expansive people feel that this WPATH recommendation restricts body autonomy. Let's take a look at what WPATH says:

> It is important for mental health professionals to recognize that decisions about surgery are first and foremost a client's decisions—as are all decisions regarding healthcare. However, mental health professionals have a responsibility to encourage, guide, and assist clients with making fully informed decisions and becoming adequately prepared. To best support their clients' decisions, mental health professionals need to have functioning working relationships with their clients and sufficient information about them. Clients should receive prompt and attentive evaluation, with the goal of alleviating their gender dysphoria and providing them with appropriate medical services. (Coleman *et al.*, 2012, p.25)

While the intention of this standard reflects a client's right to make autonomous decisions, the *need* for an "evaluation" of any kind appears to negate this. Can clinicians respect that "decisions about surgery are first and foremost a client's decisions" while being gatekeepers? Should mental health clinicians be the ones to decide whether medical interventions are necessary or contraindicated?

An example is helpful here. We consulted with a clinician who refused to provide such a letter to one client because, in the clinician's view, the client needed to "slow down" the transition process. This client was an adult seeking hormones from an endocrinology practice that required a letter of support. The client clearly understood the risks and benefits of hormones and had significant long-standing gender dysphoria. The clinician was concerned that the client would "regret" the decision to begin hormones. The client went on to seek out an endocrinology practice that did not require letters for hormones. He did not return to therapy. In the end, the clinician was unhappy with how she had handled this situation and wanted to understand whether another approach would have been better.

This case raises a number of issues. This clinician was not a gender therapist and did not fully understand how critical hormones were in alleviating this client's long-standing gender dysphoria. The client likely felt misunderstood and unsupported. However, at the other end of the spectrum, some clinicians provide letters for medical procedures based on very little information and no relationship with clients.

Differences in medical transition practices are also seen among medical providers. Some endocrinologists require letters, some do not. Some surgeons ask that clinicians follow the format for letters outlined by WPATH, others ask for different documentation. Most insurance companies require pre-authorization (including mental health letters) in order to pay for surgery.

Given these challenges, we simply try to do our best and work with clients to support their needs. An example of this lies in our work with Albert, the trans man mentioned earlier in this chapter.

Albert sought help to assist with exploring his gender identity, resolving binge eating, and managing depression. When Albert started therapy, he knew he was transgender but was uncertain about medical transition. Albert scheduled an appointment with an endocrinologist to understand hormone options. The waiting time for an appointment was three months. In that time, Albert developed a list of questions that he could ask the doctor. His provider did not require a letter of support for hormones. When the day arrived, Albert met with the doctor and brought the list of questions. He obtained the prescription for testosterone and decided to wait before filling it because of anxieties about transition. When Albert felt fully ready, he filled the prescription.

Maria is a 45-year-old trans woman. She had been on Social Security disability benefits. From the initial session, Maria was clear about her desire for top surgery. Her insurance company had strict guidelines, requiring letters to pay for surgery. When Maria hit a roadblock in seeking a surgeon within her network, she reached out to colleagues for a recommendation. Maria's insurance company required letters from two clinicians, but she was unable to afford to consult with another provider. A colleague saw Maria at a lowered cost. Following surgery, Maria felt more confident in her appearance and while she still had some difficulties with emotional eating, it was much better than it had been.

These examples show why our role is more ally than a gatekeeper. While letters of support are necessary in many cases, we work to support clients in obtaining the information and resources they need.

Another challenge with strict adherence to the *Standards of Care* is that they do not provide guidance for supporting clients who do not seek gender confirmation through medical transition. Some clients may not wish to or are unable to medically transition. Similarly, the *Standards of Care* strongly encourage providers to diagnose clients they see with gender dysphoria. Letters for hormones and surgeries require "persistent, well-documented gender dysphoria." While most of our clients meet criteria for gender dysphoria, some do not. Can clients without this diagnosis access medical services? Should the diagnosis be required? This is an area that continues to evolve.

Capacity for consent

Returning to the discussion of informed consent, we explore the role of therapist in assessing the client's capacity to give consent. For most clients, this is easily affirmed during the first session. Are they aware and oriented to person, place, time, and situation? Are they sober? A small but significant minority of clients are more challenging in this regard. Many clients have complicating presenting issues, such as those with dissociative identity disorder and active addiction.

Derek is a transgender college student who contacted us with interest in gender-confirmation surgery. During his initial session, Derek shared that he struggled with drinking too much—daily binge drinking resulted in blacking out. The primary impetus for his drinking was the pain associated with being in his body. Surgery was Derek's ultimate goal. Derek would often come to sessions drunk, and it was difficult to assess whether he fully understood the risks and benefits of surgery. In order to proceed, he would need to reduce or abstain from drinking. Derek entered an inpatient treatment program with the goal of becoming more prepared for medical transition.

While Derek demonstrated awareness of his destructive patterns, his active alcoholism prevented him from being a candidate for any type of major surgery. Derek was able to work on these behaviors and was able to proceed with surgery.

What about kids?

Consent is more complicated when the client is under the age of 18. Laws vary by state regarding medical treatment that teenagers can access without parental permission or notification. We encourage you to verify with your state regulatory boards and review your state laws to know what ages can and cannot offer consent.

For medical interventions, the WPATH *Standards of Care* require the client to be the "age of majority in a given country" (i.e., an adult) or "the adolescent has given informed consent and, particularly when the adolescent has not reached the age of medical consent, the parents or other caretakers or guardians have consented to the treatment and are involved in supporting the adolescent throughout the treatment process" (Coleman *et al.*, 2012, p.34).

Many adolescent clients will have the support and consent of their parents or guardians to move forward with gender confirmation. Some clients will not. The next chapter provides more information about family support. What do you think the experience is like for those with the support of their family? How will it differ for those without the support of their family?

FOR FURTHER EXPLORATION

- This section listed many of the benefits of transition (social, medical, legal). As you read the chapter, do other benefits come to mind? Are there any drawbacks or concerns?

- Imagine a scenario where you would need to pursue a legal name change. Take a moment to reflect on the areas of your life that would be affected. Jot down the list of things that would need to change to support your new name.

- Reflect back on the section about gatekeeping. What are your thoughts on this topic? How do you balance the need to support clients seeking letters of support with the professional ethics of your field? Do you consider yourself gatekeeper or ally?

Chapter 11

Family Support

"I wasn't in favor of the surgery. I thought, 'What if she changes her mind? We can't undo this.' All that disappeared when I saw my son after the surgery. He had the biggest smile I'd ever seen. If I ever doubted the importance of transition, I believe it now." (Father of a 30-year-old trans male)

"It wasn't about gender. We didn't subscribe to gender norms. I loved Ash as a girl and I would as a boy. But physically transition? I was scared. What if he went to college and met the wrong person at a party? What if someone found out and hurt him because he was trans? My brain will not stop. I have always tried to protect Ash." (Gwen, mother of Ash, a 17-year-old teen trans male)

"I just don't get it. Gender fluid? He should just pick a lane." (Father of a newly out gender-fluid teen)

"He wanted to be called 'Stella.' I told him it's an awful name." (Julia, mother of eight-year-old Gavin)

"If he [preferred pronoun] told other people in the family that he was a woman trapped in a man's body, they wouldn't understand. They would disown him. It's against our religion. I'm the only one who understands. It's really hard. I've finally met my life partner, and he is a she. I will be there for him as best I can." (Sara, partner to Jim—see Chapter 1)

These quotes represent some of the myriad perspectives and struggles of family members as they grapple with change: different gender identities; new names and language; challenges to the gender binary; and acceptance of bodies in transition.

Families fulfill many functions throughout the life cycle. They provide education and teach children and adolescents values. They are the first teachers and role models of gender and gender roles. Thus, they can normalize—or pathologize—their gender-diverse family members. Research shows that supportive families can promote resilience: a gender-expansive person's risk of depression and suicide diminish exponentially with the support of at least one family member. In fact, de Vries *et al.* (2014) found that with combined medical, psychological, and family care, the psychological functioning of transgender adolescents is indistinguishable from the general population of adolescents. While family support is particularly critical for children and adolescents (who are coming out at earlier ages), it is also helpful for our clients in their 30s, 40s, and beyond.

Years ago, many therapists worked from the assumption that families would reject their LGBT members and that "family" could be found *only* among the LGBT community. That is not the case. Yes, the LGBT community is generally welcoming, but acceptance from the client's family of origin is powerful. Family responses to learning that a member is transgender range from highly rejecting to highly accepting (Ryan & Chen-Hayes, 2013). Some families demonstrate a combination of accepting and rejecting behaviors. In a therapy session in which one of our trans male clients came out to his mother, she kept repeating that she was "shocked," but "loves him." While we could empathize with her surprise, her language was alternately accepting and rejecting. This mother was able to see that and changed her word choices. In another example of conflicting behaviors, a father supported his trans daughter in seeking hormones, but insisted on calling her by her birth name rather than her preferred name.

Acceptance can be a process. Adjusting to changes that may be part of transition—including body alterations—is not always easy. In her memoir, *A Little Thing Called Life*, Linda Thompson (2016), Caitlyn Jenner's first wife and the mother of Jenner's children, eloquently describes her journey in understanding Jenner's desire to transition. As Thompson was trying to wrap her mind around the idea that her virile decathlete husband was trapped in the wrong body, Jenner was much further on in this process. At one point on a weekend getaway, Jenner greeted Thompson "dressed as Caitlyn." Thompson's response was not graceful—she quickly exited the hotel. In this moment, Thompson understood the totality of what

Jenner's transition would entail. Thompson ultimately decided to end the relationship. Thompson and Jenner have since forged a new relationship and are good friends. Thompson recognizes that Jenner is far happier as Caitlyn, and Caitlyn is a much more loving parent and good friend in this contented form. Their family structure has changed, but this change is for the better.

While Thompson's experience is not meant to reflect all family's experiences, it demonstrates that there are often bumps before families find their way. This chapter will discuss the importance of family support for transgender and gender-expansive clients. We will discuss common reactions of family members and present guidelines for support. As in other chapters, we will share our clients' experiences and voices.

Importance of family support

What have you seen as families struggle with other challenges, such as learning that a member is abusing substances, has lost a job, or is gay or lesbian? It is likely that their responses are varied.

Families react differently when they learn that a son, daughter, or partner is gender expansive or transgender or wants to transition. These reactions range from unconditional acceptance to outright rejection. Often, the response is somewhere in between. Families may express surprise or confusion, question whether the person is sure, use words that are emotionally charged (shocked, devastated), or express disbelief. It is helpful to discuss this range of responses with clients beforehand and to normalize it. Similarly, questions arise when a family member begins to look at physical transition, such as hormones or surgery. They may ask if the family member is certain they want to transition, or question whether the person can "change back" after transition. Families may express particular fears related to career aspirations or college choices. For example, Randy was a singer. Randy's mother, Lisa, was adamantly against Randy beginning testosterone because of the potential for changes to Randy's voice. Most families genuinely want what's best for their family member. Lisa was not questioning Randy's gender identity, but she was afraid that 12 years' worth of voice training would be "wasted."

Family responses are also influenced by the family's own unique lens. And that lens may not be rainbow colored. It's important to meet family members where they are and to support their understanding of what will allow their family member to flourish. Gender dysphoria could present with early signs or without any signs until the onset of puberty.

It's important to ensure that families understand the harmful effects of rejection. Young adults rejected by families are more likely to be significantly depressed (or suicidal), to abuse substances (including food), and to engage in risky behaviors (Ryan, 2009). Our client Andy, for example, was subjected to repeated bullying at home and pressures from parents to embrace his femininity. Andy was also discriminated against and bullied on the job. When he quit, Andy was left with no income and no family to buffer against minority stress (work discrimination). Andy moved in with a man who provided shelter in return for sex. Andy felt that this was preferable to living with his parents. Following an episode of severe depression and a suicide attempt, Andy received help and found genuinely safe LGBT housing. This allowed him to develop strong bonds and a "family of creation" that was fully affirming.

Loss versus individual and family resilience

Gwen (quoted in the introduction to this chapter) is the mother of Ash, who is 17. Ash came out at 15, first as gender fluid and, over the last six months, as a trans male. Some facets of the social transition were difficult. "I cried when Ash cut his beautiful hair," Gwen says, "but I could immediately see how much more confident Ash became." It was also difficult for Gwen to put away old pictures of Ash. To Ash, this signified that Gwen preferred his former physical appearance.

Ash began discussing his desire for top surgery. Gwen noticed her own anxiety increase, and acknowledged that the possibility of surgery had made Ash's transition more "real" for her. Gwen's anxiety appeared to be fear-based: "Ash was a strong female but would be a vulnerable male." Gwen, herself the survivor of a sexual assault, was concerned that physical transition would increase Ash's risk of victimization.

Gwen decided to seek therapeutic support to work on resolving her own trauma. She also asked Ash if she could be involved in his college research, to help him identify schools that were LGBT-affirming and safe. While she is still nervous, she feels more in control and has been a constant ally to Ash.

Gwen's story illustrates that challenges can occur when families are at different points in a member's gender journey. Over time, Gwen struggled with various aspects of Ash's transition—such as cutting his hair—but other things were not problematic. Gwen never questioned his need to transition socially or change his name or pronoun. When we asked Gwen about the stressful points in Ash's transition (even the most recent ones), she saw these as adaptations to change and within the realm of what could be expected when raising an independent, assertive teen.

People sometimes compare the experience of families learning that a loved one is transgender to the loss of a close family member. Using grief and loss as an analogy is well meaning (and still widely used), but we do not think that it is the best way to look at gender concerns. Yes, families often react with strong emotions (including sadness, anger, guilt, or disbelief), and they may try to bargain with the person ("Just wait, don't move ahead too quickly and...")—all of which are parts of traditional models of grieving. While using a grief analogy can provide comfort to some families, we believe that a better way to look at this process is as a type of family adaptation or family resilience.

Simply put, resilience is the process of acclimatizing to challenging situations. Being resilient, however, does not mean that people do not experience difficulty or even distress. Families come to therapy with unique histories and challenges, but also with multiple assets and resources. These resources allow them to adjust to changes within the family system.

In learning that a family member is gender diverse, there are many adaptations to be made. Consider just a few of these: coping with adolescence as a whole (and the capricious nature of teens); understanding that gender is internal; learning new pronouns and one or more new names; getting used to clothing and physical changes such as shorter or longer hair; and seeking competent medical providers. As with Gwen, various points in transition may bring up different feelings, but the feeling that things are in a state of flux does settle down as the family member continues with his/her/their transition.

Many factors contribute to resilience, such as reactivity to stress, temperament, prior experiences of coping and adaptation, life circumstances, cultural and religious influences, and perceptions of control. These family variables include:

- family openness and genuine communication
- family ability to adapt to change
- overall family health and well-being
- family resourcefulness and creativity
- commitment to one another
- bonding and respect
- family problem-solving skills.

While many of these traits are established, others (e.g., better communication) can be built. Gwen and Ash demonstrate many of these resiliency traits. They were committed to one another and had already been through adaptation to Ash's identification as gender fluid. One of the biggest assets in this family was its wonderful problem-solving skills. Gwen's ability to feel safer by researching safety and support at various local colleges was beneficial to her family. In fact, Gwen put together a written guide with her findings and has offered it to her local PFLAG chapter. This benefitted other families in the college-search process.

Family adjustment and resilience is not just confined to families of teens; age is not a limitation in family resiliency. Sara, who is quoted at the outset of this chapter, was in her late 50s when her life partner, Jim, disclosed his longing to be a woman. Sara, too, demonstrates factors that define resilience.

The daughter of a Holocaust survivor and an observant Jew, Sara had a childhood that was challenging because of her father's emotional distance. Our initial work in therapy focused on this. Her father, who by then was elderly, was experiencing chronic health issues. Sara found it difficult to adapt to her father's illness and to forgive him for his shortcomings, but finally being able to do so was extremely cathartic to her.

After her father's death, Sara began to talk more about her relationship with Jim. When she met him, Jim initially reminded her of a "more earthy" version of her father. Jim was very masculine and "rough" at times. The couple has always communicated well with one another.

Sara was initially devastated when Jim shared his thoughts about feeling "trapped" by his masculine self. Jim had not shared his gender diversity with anyone else in his life. At times, Sara was extremely angry—especially when Jim would wear feminine clothing or make comments about coveting parts of her body. As Sara's anger gave way to sadness and empathy, Jim began to share more himself. Sara got to know his more sensitive and nurturing side.

Sara described "falling in love all over again" with this sensitive and nurturing person. Sara made the connection that this nurturing part of Jim was his feminine self. Sara's acceptance increased exponentially as they attended conjoint sessions. In addition to working with us, Jim and Sara also met regularly with a Reconstructionist rabbi, whom a friend recommended. The rabbi was non-judgmental and did not endorse the same religious prohibitions as their more conservative rabbi. The secular and rabbinical counseling helped them to work through the complexities of being coupled when one member is gender diverse.

Jim feels that transitioning physically could never be acceptable to his wider family circle, so he has no plans to do so. This both saddens and reassures Sara. She is uncertain how she will react if Jim should ever decide to move ahead with hormones or surgery, but she doesn't feel as if it would be something she could never tolerate. Sara also sometimes feels anger that Jim's secret can be burdensome.

As with Gwen and Ash, Sara and Jim's process was not always smooth. There were many emotional sessions. While the two eventually were able to find some degree of equanimity, they were aware that the challenges associated with physical transition—should Jim ever proceed with it—may or may not be surmountable.

Assumptions in working with families

Julia and Kevin are the parents of Gavin, who is eight and in second grade. They are in their late 40s. Kevin works in the financial services industry and Julia is a stay-at-home mother. Prior to becoming pregnant with Gavin, Julia was laid off from a high-income job. Julia enjoys being off the fast track, although she recognizes that living on a single income creates a financial strain for the family.

Since about the age of five, Gavin has expressed that he is a girl. While Julia and Kevin want what's best for Gavin, they struggle to address Gavin's gender concerns. They have not told their extended family about Gavin's preferred gender and allow him to wear girl's clothing only at home. When Gavin was invited to a friend's swim party, however, Julia went to a significant amount of effort to seek out pink swim trunks. She was upset that Gavin was not more appreciative and that he continued to ask about wearing a girl's swimsuit.

At a recent appointment with the pediatrician, the doctor noticed that Julia was struggling and suggested that she seek support. Gavin's pediatrician also recently suggested a referral to a gender clinic to learn more about puberty blockers and physical transition, which was something that they would soon need to consider. While that was difficult, the main precipitant was Gavin's request to be called Stella. "I told him it's an awful name," Julia states.

In working with families like Julia and Kevin, we find that a number of things guide the work of facilitating acceptance and support within the family system.

Family knowledge, expectations, and beliefs

Families come into therapy with many assumptions about gender. They also come to us with beliefs that affect their ideas about the gender binary, gender role, and assigned sex. While some families that seek counseling are extremely supportive and knowledgeable about gender diversity and need minimal guidance, others have more limited information.

In our initial session with a client, we assess family knowledge, expectations, and beliefs. Some of the following questions are helpful:

- What brought you here today? How do you think therapy can be helpful?

- What is your understanding of your family member's gender identity?

- What are your beliefs about boys/men? Girls/women?

- Do you believe that gender must be binary?

- Has your family member's gender diversity created any stress within your family?

- What is the most important thing you have learned about [preferred name's] gender identity so far?

- What next steps are you considering? Are there things that could get in the way of these steps (e.g., fears that it is a phase)?

- What do you need help in navigating regarding your son/daughter/spouse's gender identity?

Take a multigenerational approach

In addition to considering the nuclear family and where it is, it helps to look at the wider family system. How is the extended family able to integrate and accept gender differences? In taking a multi-generational approach, consider using tried-and-true tools, such as family genograms. Genograms (invented by Murray Bowen) are family trees that go back several generations. While genograms can capture many kinds of information, patterns related to approval, tolerance, and change can be enlightening. For example, has the extended family navigated changes previously? Has it experienced an inter-racial or inter-religious marriage? Has there been a family member who is or was gay or lesbian? Has someone left the family's predominant religion? The traditional genogram structure can be easily adapted to be inclusive of nonbinary gender identities in the family system. For example, you can choose a symbol, such as "N," to represent a nonbinary identity.

We include questions about traditional attitudes within the family and across generations. Some families, for example, see women's bodies as the major source of esteem or something that makes them more attractive to a mate. Thus, an assigned female's desire to transition to male may be difficult to comprehend, as the family member is giving up a major source of currency. Religious, spiritual, and cultural issues connected to gender and identity are also key. These factors provide clues about how the family may adjust to transition. Questions about family secrets are closely related. These may involve any of the subjects above—or more taboo topics, such as family traumas or addictive behaviors. Including this information in the genogram helps clients externalize these issues and reduce emotional reactivity.

While there are many possible areas to include (and please expand on these below if you sense something relevant), the following questions can be helpful. Even if you do not use a genogram, this information can help expand your understanding of family dynamics.

- What is your extended family's cultural background?

- What role did religious or spiritual beliefs play within the extended family?

- What does this religious, spiritual, or cultural tradition say about gender? Sexuality?

- Have there been instances in which family members have engaged in behaviors that may have seemed counter to religious or cultural beliefs or traditions? What are some examples?

- Has your family encountered things such as intermarriage? A family member that is gay/lesbian or bisexual? How have they responded?

- What are gender roles like in your family? Traditional? Non-traditional? Flexible? Rigid?

- Have members of your family had any major mental illnesses, including alcoholism, addiction, or eating disorders? Are they discussed openly or transformed into family secrets?

- What are the prevailing body norms in your family (e.g., norms that say women must be thin or an acceptance of all body shapes and sizes)? Do these differ based on gender?

- What family secrets are you aware of (consider taboos such as traumas, unplanned pregnancies or adoptions, or infidelity)?

Know that intentions are generally positive, and practice neutrality

In most cases, family members' intentions are positive. Even in families where issues have seemed egregious or unable to be bridged, intentions are often positive.

It may not be feasible to achieve family support in all instances. In families with especially rigid boundaries, acceptance may not be possible. In these cases, we work with clients individually to understand that they need to create a different support system. Dialectics can help ("My family is very religious and cannot accept my gender identity. While they love me, they are not emotionally safe. I cannot maintain this relationship").

Julia and Kevin's stance about Gavin's gender identity was a test of therapeutic neutrality. They did not want to share Gavin's gender identity with his grandparents because of their doubts that it would be acceptable within their religiously conservative extended family. While they wanted Gavin to have a relationship with grandparents, they knew that Gavin could be rejected. The family chose to cut off these relationships, fearing that Gavin could be harmed by them.

We also discussed Gavin's request to change his name. Julia was able to share that her strong reaction to the name "Stella" was because of a family member named Stella who tormented her as a child—and that hearing the name brought back bad memories. This opened the door for negotiation. About a year into treatment, Julia, Kevin, and Gavin sat down with a name book together. They chose to look at names beginning with "S" to honor Gavin's original preference. Together the family selected the name "Sage," which means "wise." Sage adored her new name, one that worked for all of them.

Provide an open, non-judgmental space for all

Closely related to practicing neutrality is the idea of a non-judgmental space. If family members feel as if they cannot not verbalize their concerns (and be heard objectively) in the therapy space, then how can they model the same for their gender-diverse family member? We often get to know our clients individually, and based on what they share about family support, comments from other family members, and our own interactions with their families, assess what form family intervention should take. Some options are: no family therapy needed or only limited contact with the individual therapist; family therapy with all members; parents separate; and parents in separate individual therapy.

There may be value in having a separate therapy space for different family members. Many of the couples we work with, for example, have their own therapists. For parent/child combinations, we often see the transgender family member separately and come together as a family at strategic intervals. This allows all family members to be in on the conversation, yet it still supports the unedited verbalization of positive and negative feelings and reactions. In some cases, separate individual therapy is valuable. Sara, for example, needed individual therapy to work on her reactions to her father (and Jim reminded her of her father). Gwen had trauma processing to do. When possible, collaboration between all clinicians—working toward a common goal of family support—is key.

In inviting family members to participate in therapy, you gain a much fuller picture of the client and the overall family dynamic. In meeting with parents or partners independently, we found that they would often sigh and say, "Thank goodness I can say what I need rather than trying to be sensitive all the time." Separate space is also a place for them to ask the questions that teens in particular do not tolerate well.

One example that comes to mind is a parent who brought an article on detransition into family therapy with their child present. Thomas, a trans teen, saw it as a rejection and a communication that he was "not really trans." We supported the parents in expressing their fears about how transition would affect body changes, and educated them about how infrequently detransition occurred. Alternately, Thomas was able to express that the article made him doubt his parents' support and scared him about moving ahead with medical transition. After talking through these differing perspectives, the family was able to better support Thomas in taking the steps he needed to take.

Educate, educate, educate

Psychoeducation, formal or informal, can be very helpful. This includes book recommendations, educational groups (such as Trans 101), and referring families to PFLAG meetings and community events.

Another form of education is asking about (and debunking) myths about being transgender. Here are some common myths:

- Gender is universal and must be binary.

- A parent somehow "caused" their child to become transgender.

- All transgender people lead unhappy lives.

- Transgender people cannot be accepted by society and that they will be isolated, ostracized, and unsafe.

- There is a one-size-fits-all transition.

- A person cannot be transgender if there were no "warning signs" in early childhood.

- Medical transition is a must.

- Being transgender is a fad.

- Being transgender is a rejection of the family values or a rebellion.

- Transgender people are likely to detransition.

- Sexual orientation changes with gender changes.

Julia and Kevin, Gavin's parents, had many of these misconceptions about gender identity, and we addressed them through a combination of reading assignments and by answering questions (and more questions). At the PFLAG group, they were able to meet and talk with other parents of trans children. These parents were a wealth of information and support for Julia and Kevin.

One of the obstacles to Julia and Kevin more fully supporting Gavin (who had not yet chosen the name "Sage") was Julia's belief that she had somehow "caused" Gavin's gender preferences. Julia felt guilty that she had somehow failed in her job as a mother. Directly addressing the guilt and assuring Julia that she had not caused Gavin to be trans was a turning point for the family.

Help families widen their support networks

As Julia and Kevin learned, support from other families can also be very beneficial. In addition to PFLAG, many local gender clinics and hospitals have parent support groups. One of the benefits of a group like PFLAG is that families can see others who are at similar stages of acceptance as they are and some who may be further along. PFLAG welcomes all family members across all ages—parents, grandparents, siblings, and others. Groups like PFLAG reduce isolation and provide support.

Frequently, spouses and partners also feel isolated. Resources specific to them include the Straight Spouse Network (support for spouses/partners of trans people) and COLAGE (support for people whose parents are trans or queer).

FOR FURTHER EXPLORATION

- Imagine a significant, difficult, or challenging experience in your own family. How did you approach this difficulty (e.g., through educating them, seeking the support of one member, calling a family meeting)? What was helpful? What would you change?

- Create a genogram for your family. Go back at least two generations if possible. Looking at the patterns you note, how do you predict your family would react to a transgender family member? If you already have a transgender family member, what has their support been like? What are some of the factors you see in the genogram that seem to drive those reactions?

- Look at the list of myths about gender identity. If a family member shared that they believed one of these myths, how would you respond? What evidence could you present to counter the myth?

Chapter 12

Barriers to Treatment

Ari, a 55-year-old trans male client, has known about his gender identity since his teens and has struggled with binging and purging since that time. Ari has been socially and medically transitioning for more than a year and is happier in his body since beginning the transition. His decision to transition, however, led to the breakup of a long-standing relationship with his partner. Ari also lost his job as a nurse and believes that his inability to find another position is related to his gender identity. Lately, Ari has felt more depressed and is questioning whether the transition has been worth the losses. Ari's binging and purging, which had been relatively stable since transition, is steadily worsening. He has contacted multiple programs that do not anticipate openings, cannot work with transgender males, or do not take his insurance. As treatment options narrow, his hopelessness and eating-disorder symptoms increase.

Ari's story illustrates the many difficulties when referring clients for eating-disorder care. These obstacles can often feel insurmountable. If we are disheartened by this, our clients are even more so. And while there is some improvement, change is slow.

What came up for you while reading Ari's story? Have you had similar experiences when seeking programs for your clients?

The clinical world we know most intimately is within the field of eating disorders. In this chapter, we identify and address many of the barriers that gender-expansive clients have when accessing treatment for eating disorders. While some of the barriers (such as lack of weight norms for gender-diverse clients) are specific to the care of eating disorders, others (such as lack of training and sensitivity) apply to many settings.

Not all eating-disorder programs are equal in terms of care, and not all are suitable for working with gender-expansive clients. To assess eating-disorder care, we ask a number of questions. Does the program support clients with diverse bodies? Does it work with all eating disorders? Does its nutritional philosophy mirror our own? Does the program have an understanding of trauma-informed care and co-occurring disorders? If these concepts are new to you, you will likely recognize that specialized knowledge is required to work effectively with gender-expansive clients who also have eating disorders.

If a program passes this initial screen, we listen for details that indicate its approach to working with clients who are transgender and gender expansive. Does the program use preferred names and pronouns? Are there housing options that clients will feel comfortable with? What type of experience do they have working with trans clients? Are there red flags that could represent bias or discrimination?

As with Ari, clients seeking treatment for eating disorders encounter many challenges, including gender-specific programming, insurance and financial limitations, and housing concerns. Other barriers include a lack of transgender-specific services and little to no staff training on gender issues. Some clients have entered programs that seemed appropriate, only to have negative experiences. Let's look more closely at these issues.

Which level of care is needed?

Andrea is a 16-year-old client who identifies as agender (she uses she/her pronouns). Andrea had been struggling with her gender identity. She had become increasingly depressed and suicidal at times. Recently, she had sharply restricted her food intake. Andrea had lost a significant amount of weight (45 pounds in a three-month period). While Andrea's body mass index would still be considered within normal range, Andrea's skin color did not look good and her fatigue was obvious. A glance at her Fitbit showed that her heart rate was in the low 40s.

Andrea's story provides a glimpse into the psychiatric and medical complexity of clients with eating disorders. If you had a client such as Andrea in your practice, where would you send her for treatment?

Levels of care

- *Inpatient hospitals* are suitable for clients who are medically unstable and need the care of a physician and medical staff in addition to mental health clinicians. Clients are usually closely monitored to minimize use of eating-disorder behaviors and promote medical improvement. Clients are housed onsite, monitored by doctors and nurses. For clients whose weight is too low, weight gain is a goal of inpatient treatment.

- *Residential settings* are appropriate for clients who are medically stable but have been hospitalized multiple times. Clients in residential settings live onsite, often in apartment-style, shared housing. They can attend therapeutic programming and engage in activities that mirror outside life, such as cooking and grocery shopping. The goal is to allow easier re-entry to home and reduction of eating-disorder symptoms.

- *Partial hospitalization,* or day treatment programs, offer clinical services for clients who do not live onsite. The clients in this level of care are more medically stable, need less intensive therapy, and are less psychiatrically complex than those requiring inpatient or residential care. Clients attend day treatment programming, daily, for between eight and ten hours. They are also monitored to ensure medical stability.

- *Intensive outpatient programs* provide clinical services for a range of 9–15 hours a week. Clients in intensive outpatient programs are expected to be self-sufficient in their recovery when outside the program. Best-practice treatment for eating disorders involves individual therapy, nutrition therapy, medical monitoring, and psychiatric care.

- *Outpatient services* are offered on a once to twice weekly basis. Some clients will attend an outpatient clinical group or a local eating-disorder recovery support group, or will participate in meal support at their provider's office, or engage in an in-home meal support program.

All of these settings of care have unique challenges for working effectively with gender-expansive clients. Before discussing these challenges let's look at access to services.

Barriers to accessing care

To be successful in eating-disorder treatment, clients need first to be able to access services. While that sounds as if it should be relatively simple, for transgender and gender-expansive clients, accessing care can be a feat. Ari's situation highlighted some of the common problems our clients encounter. Let's look more closely at other barriers to care.

Role of gender

Eating disorders have historically been viewed as a "women's issue." As such, many programs only accept female clients. How does the program define "woman"? Would a transfeminine client be welcome? A nonbinary client?

Thapliyal, Hay, and Conti (2018) looked at the role of gender in the treatment experiences of people with eating disorders. Their study was an analysis of other research. Among the data they analyzed were qualitative studies of the treatment experiences of women, men, and people who identify along the LGBT spectrum. These researchers identified a number of themes relevant to the eating-disorder treatment process:

- For women, treatment was often viewed through the lens of gender (Robinson, Mountford, & Sperlinger, 2013). This included female-specific programs and groups.

- Three was bias toward the idea that eating disorders are only a woman's issue (Holmes, 2016).

- Eating disorders are underdiagnosed in men.

- There are problems associated with "erasing" gender in treatment; gender is important in looking at trans-specific concerns (Duffy, Henkel, & Earnshaw, 2016).

- Many providers are not literate in gender-related issues and needs (Robinson *et al.*, 2013).

- Decisions not to disclose gender identity (Duffy *et al.*, 2016).

One frustration, especially when referring gender-expansive clients to a higher level of care (such as inpatient), is with female-only programs that do not have appropriate protocols for transgender or nonbinary clients. At times, these are the only available choice.

Bry, a 25-year-old gender-nonbinary client with bulimia, entered a women's eating disorder program. It was the only local option covered by their (preferred pronoun) insurance. The admissions team was willing to accept Bry, since they were assigned female at birth. Bry left treatment two days later. The assumptions and content of a women's program did not address Bry's experiences. Staff members routinely misgendered Bry and did not use Bry's preferred pronoun. Bry's eating disorder felt "different" from the other people in the program. Bry could not really open up in an environment that assumed everyone was female.

Sarah, a 20-year-old transfeminine client with binge eating disorder, also attended a women-only program. She connected well with her therapist, who was clearly trans-competent, and she felt welcomed throughout treatment. Staff and clients seemed interested in learning about Sarah's life and were supportive of her struggles in gaining acceptance in the larger world. While she was initially anxious about the program, she had a positive experience.

Gender-specific programs can be a powerful option for some clients, although they are not for everyone. In Sarah's case, a number of factors contributed to her success in the program. This included the affirming nature of the program and its definition of "gender" and "female" that went beyond birth sex. Sara left the program with a sense of belonging, and her symptoms were more stable.

Gendered approaches to eating-disorder treatment may not be an appropriate option for all of our clients, including some who identify as nonbinary. Over the last few years, the number of co-ed programs offering services for both men and women has increased. This opens the door for transgender clients to enter treatment more easily, but it does not guarantee staff competence. A handful of programs promote their services as being for clients of all genders. An increasing number of facilities seem to be expanding their ability to serve the gender-expansive community. Imagine, for example, how Bry's experience could have been different if they attended a program that was both welcoming and competent in providing treatment for nonbinary clients with eating disorders.

Lack of training or competence, discrimination

One of the primary barriers to treatment involves a lack of training or competence in treating gender-expansive people (Safer *et al.*, 2016). This is an evolving field and it will take time to bridge gaps in training. Until then, it is important to acknowledge programmatic lack of competence ("We are not properly trained in working with gender-expansive clients") rather than to imply that something is wrong with the client ("We don't work with clients like you"). Closely connected with this lack of competence is the misunderstanding and discrimination trans people face due to this lack of training.

At times, lack of training and competence is evident in client interactions. This limits the number of programs we can safely refer to. It also adds to client trauma. Consider Myra, a transfeminine client early in her transition, who was asked for her "gender preference" by a well-meaning intake counselor. The phrase "gender preference" unintentionally perpetuates the belief that being transgender or gender diverse is a choice. A person's gender identity is not a preference—it is who they are.

Felix's situation was even more tricky.

Felix is a 23-year-old trans male client with anorexia and post-traumatic stress disorder who needed to be hospitalized for medical and psychiatric stabilization. We identified a program that would work with Felix's insurance and began the intake process. The intake was running smoothly until Felix shared that he was transgender. The intake counselor at first stumbled over her words, and then said it was the program's policy to provide single rooms for transgender clients. The intake person was unsure when the next single room would be open. When assured that Felix was comfortable sharing a room with another man, we were met with a stony silence from the intake person, who responded, "We'll call when a single room opens up."

Three weeks passed without an update from the program on Felix's status on the waiting list. We learned of another therapist's cisgender client being admitted to the program despite completing the intake a week after Felix. When we called to follow-up, we were finally told by a program administrator that the treatment team did not think Felix was appropriate for its program because he would likely need "more support" than other clients. They cited his hormone regimen as outside the scope of what they could provide.

Insurance-related concerns, inequitable coverage

All insurance plans have limitations unique to their own coverage policies and benefit structures. Benefit designs, the scope of provider networks, and staff training all represent plan-level impediments to needed services (Safer *et al.*, 2016). Such impediments can occur due to:

- limits in coverage or lack of coverage for certain levels of care (such as not having a residential benefit)

- coverage for treatment at specific facilities that may or may not be trans competent

- pre-authorization by staff who do not understand the complexities of eating disorder or trans care

- co-insurance rates that are so high that clients cannot access services.

These limitations are common in commercial health plans, but tend to be even more present for government-sponsored health plans, such as Medicare and Medicaid. Transgender clients often live in poverty. The National Transgender Discrimination Survey (Grant *et al.*, 2011) found that respondents were nearly four times more likely than the general population to have a household income of less than $10,000 per year. Clients who are economically disadvantaged are typically reliant on Medicare or Medicaid or have only basic private insurance. This makes it difficult to refer clients for care, especially to programs that are trans competent.

Denver, for example, is a 33-year-old transfeminine client who has struggled with bulimia for more than 20 years. She has been hospitalized many times. Denver struggles to find in-network providers, let alone trans-affirmative providers. Recently, Denver needed inpatient hospitalization for medical stabilization of her eating disorder. It is often difficult to find programs willing to take her insurance. The only hospital willing to work with us had a program that Denver had previously attended and reported numerous adverse experiences once the staff learned she was transgender. The insurance representative was unmoved by Denver's prior experiences. The plan refused to pay for another program. We ultimately chose to try to stabilize Denver in an outpatient setting—which was difficult but more compassionate.

Economic barriers

Economic challenges can also be a barrier to appropriate care. Examples are numerous and range from out-of-pocket expenses to concerns about trade-offs between being able to afford treatment and the everyday cost of living. Many specialists in eating disorders and trans health are self-pay only. They may or may not offer services on a sliding scale.

As mentioned previously, many transgender clients live on minimal incomes, and for these individuals, every penny counts. Transportation costs may limit the distance that clients can travel for care. Some clients rely on public transportation or van services offered by treatment facilities. Others struggle to pay for food, rent, and utilities when the out-of-pocket costs of their treatment are substantial.

Guidelines for navigating barriers to access

Therapists can assist clients with concerns such as these by understanding a client's unique barriers to access, including insurance-based limitations. Some additional suggestions:

- Know the program options that are available and advocate for these options when needed.

- Talk with clients about preferences, concerns, and what they may encounter in gender-based programming.

- Advocate for other client needs (e.g., a single room, a trans male client in a men's program).

- If you refer to a program frequently, offer educational resources about trans-affirmative care.

- If you are an individual provider, consider offering insurance-paid services or sliding-scale payment options.

Challenges in treatment

Your client is in treatment. It's smooth sailing from now on, right? Think again.

Where do I pee? (or The Great Bathroom Challenge)

Melanie is a 17-year-old trans female who is hospitalized for the first time. Melanie is on hormones, but has not had any kind of surgery. She has bulimia, which is very connected to the body shame she feels. After lunch on the first day of treatment, Melanie asks to use the restroom. She is horrified when a female tech member accompanies her, and impatiently asks which bathroom she prefers. When Melanie points to the women's restroom, she notices the tech exchange a look with the nurse on the unit. Melanie feels even more body shame.

Bathrooms are a sensitive topic for clients in treatment for eating disorders. Depending on the level of care, bathroom use may be limited or restricted to supervised visits only. Some eating-disorder symptoms, such as purging through vomiting or laxative abuse, occur primarily in the bathroom. For that reason, many programs lock bathrooms. Others require clients to use bathrooms with staff supervision.

If the bathrooms at the program are segregated by gender, this can become an even more stressful situation for a gender-expansive client. How will the program accommodate the transgender client who is anxious about using the bathroom? Are there single-stall or family restrooms available? Will the staff member supervising bathroom use be sensitive to gender-identity issues? In Melanie's situation, the latter was not the case.

For any level of care that offers housing, such as inpatient or residential programs, bathrooms become an even more significant topic. Do clients share bathrooms in their living quarters? How are they assigned? Are there any rules about using the bathroom for showers and personal hygiene? As with regular bathroom use, many inpatient programs will require staff supervision while clients shower. For gender-expansive clients, this degree of supervision may trigger their gender dysphoria and general anxiety. For some, this can become a barrier to entering treatment.

Is there a space for me?

Inpatient and residential treatment programs have the unique challenge of providing housing for their clients. Inpatient programs are typically hospital-based, while residential programs may be in more of a home-like setting.

How are clients assigned to rooms? Does the program offer single or double bedrooms? How are housing options described to clients? If there is a roommate, how are roommates determined?

Now, let's return to Felix's story. Would his experience have been different if the treatment program offered everyone single rooms? Many eating disorder programs are realizing the benefits of single rooms and, when resources allow for it, are transforming doubles into singles for all clients—cisgender, transgender, and gender expansive—who seek services.

That's not my name! And other gendering concerns

Names are everywhere in treatment. Clients are entered into a medical record from the point of first contact. Programs typically require that staff to use the client's legal name for purposes such as the medical record, progress notes, and ID bracelets. Many of our clients have legal names that do not match their gender identities. Names can immediately out a trans client, and continued use of a client's dead name can be experienced as a microaggression.

Does the program have a place for clients to share their preferred names and pronouns? Are staff members sensitive about the use of names when interacting with clients?

In an ideal treatment world, from the moment of intake onward, clients would be asked about their preferred names *first* and their legal name second. This reinforces the importance of the chosen name to the client while also recognizing the need for a legal name for medical records. Unfortunately, some electronic medical records make this extremely difficult.

Can you think of other places where names show up in treatment? For example:

- Shift reports that use client first names.

- Bed boards that show who is in what room.

- Medical bracelets (inpatient programs).

- Roll-call lists at the start of group.

- Menus that clients complete.

- Mealtime placemats or other assigned seating lists.

- Signatures needed for insurance.

- Prescriptions and other notes from the doctor.

What weight? And how to communicate this

Another potential barrier that is unique to treatment of eating disorders involves the approach to weight restoration and identifying healthy weight ranges. Many programs use growth charts to determine ideal body weight. Others use the body mass index measure (which is inherently gendered). Almost all formulas for determining a healthy weight range are based on biological sex. What happens if the client presenting to treatment is transgender? How does the medical and nutritional team determine weight goals?

This is another area of emerging focus. While providers and programs recognize that weight goals and standards need to be altered for trans clients, especially those who are post-transition, formal guidelines have not yet caught up. When we put this question to several of the trans-affirmative physicians we know, an emerging standard appeared to be a determination of weight ranges based at least partially on medical transition. A trusted colleague stated that she uses common sense, but often defaults to growth curves for a client's natal gender early in transition. For clients who are 6–12 months into hormonal transition, the physician uses norms for the gender to which the person is transitioning.

It's helpful to have these conversations with clients, who understand that bodies may look different and be different weights. Don't assume that a client will not be in favor of a higher weight range, especially when they understand that such growth corresponds with their gender identity.

When programs do establish weight goals, how can they communicate goals in a manner that is respectful to the client's current gender identity? If there is a need to reference childhood growth patterns, what terminology and pronouns are used?

Let's demonstrate how this can look, using an example of a doctor discussing weight goals with a client. We will look at trans-affirmative and less-than-affirmative versions of the same scenario involving Shay, a teenage transmasculine client who is motivated for recovery and is discussing weight goals with his doctor:

Scenario 1: Problematic

Doctor: "You are doing well in your treatment. You should be at your discharge weight soon."

Shay: "What weight do I need to be?"

Doctor: "Well, we determined that based on the information your pediatrician sent us. When you were younger, you were progressing along these lines [points to lines on the chart]. Once your anorexia started, your weight remained flat. We need to get you back on track for girls your age, so that your periods come back. Well, you know what I mean. If not, you risk compromising your overall health, including your height and growth."

Shay: "Uh, okay," shifting uncomfortably and breaking eye contact. "What about boys my age?"

Doctor: "Oh. We'll have to see about that. The point is that you will be okay as long as you continue to gain weight. Any more questions?"

Shay: "No, thanks. Can I go now?"

Scenario 2: Trans-affirmative

Doctor: "You are doing well in your treatment. You should be at your discharge weight soon."

Shay: "What weight do I need to be?"

Doctor: "Well, we determined that based on the information your pediatrician sent us. When you were younger, you were progressing along these lines [points to lines on the chart]. Once your anorexia started, your weight remained flat. We need to get you back on track for someone your age based on this—or you risk compromising your overall health, including your height and growth."

Shay: "Oh, that's complicated. But I'll be okay healthwise?"

Doctor: "Yes, we believe you will make a strong recovery as long as you continue to progress as you are doing. Any more questions?"

Shay: "No, thanks. See you next session."

Many providers use "you" language without thinking twice. If there is a need to reference the person's childhood experience, when possible, omitting gender from the conversation will likely be most effective. Gendered pronouns and terminology (like "girl") can derail a session very quickly.

Hormones for everyone

Treatment programs need to address the specific medical needs of the transgender or gender-diverse client. Inpatient programs typically monitor and administer all medications, including hormones. For gender-expansive clients taking hormones as part of hormone replacement therapy (HRT), this is a critical issue. Will the program support the client's use of a hormone regimen? Is it possible for clients to obtain blood work, if needed, to sustain HRT? While this may seem intuitive for most providers, we have run across institutions that did not allow clients to continue their HRT while in treatment.

Felix had an adverse experience during an inpatient treatment episode regarding access to his hormones. This is common with many of our clients, who are frequently told what an "inconvenience" such a change (administering hormones) in hospital routine is. A hospital staff member mocked Felix when he requested access to his hormones, stating that this was "ridiculous" and "not part of my job." Felix was extremely upset. He filed a written complaint, but was never notified of the outcome. Other clients' experiences have ranged from uneducated to insensitive to blatantly transphobic.

Training discrepancies among clinicians

There is a significant deficit when it comes to provider knowledge about eating-disorder treatment, about working with gender-expansive clients, and about the intersection of these areas. Let's pause for a moment and check in with you regarding your own training and background.

Graduate education:

- How much time was focused on treating eating disorders?

- How much time was spent focused on treating LGBTQ clients? Of this time, how much was dedicated to gender-diverse clients?

- Was there any overlap? Did your training discuss working with transgender or gender-expansive clients with eating disorders?

- Did your field education, internship, or practicum site provide you with experience working with clients with eating disorders? Gender-diverse clients? Gender-diverse clients with disordered eating?

Continuing education and conferences:

- How many continuing education or conference credits have you obtained regarding treating clients with eating disorders?

- Of your eating-disorder continuing education opportunities, how many have included discussion and case examples with gender-expansive clients?

- How many continuing education/conference credits have you obtained regarding working with LGBTQ clients? How much of the discussion focused on transgender and gender-diverse clients?

- Of your continuing education opportunities focused on transgender and gender-expansive clients, how many included discussion about eating disorders in this population?

If you are a specialist working at the intersection of eating-disorder treatment and LGBTQ clients, thank you for what you do and the knowledge you bring to your clients. If you are like the majority of providers out there, you may have received training in one of the two areas. Maybe both areas. But rarely does training in either intersect with the other.

Eating disorder therapists

Many providers in the field of eating disorders have extensive training. At this time, however, adequate resources that contain trans-treatment guidelines are lacking.

There is a disconnect between the clinical criteria for eating disorders and the type of eating disorder manifesting in a client with co-occurring gender dysphoria. Many clients anchor their body-image disturbances to the gendered aspects of body—chest, facial features, hips, and overall body shape. These clients connect more with body shame or hatred related to specific body parts rather than the traditional weight-based fears.

How can we bring these two worlds together? There are many opportunities for learning. We hope that eating-disorder treatment programs will consider attending and being represented at conferences targeting professionals who specialize in LGBTQ issues, and that LGBTQ-specialized programs will be present at conferences focused on eating disorders treatment.

FOR FURTHER EXPLORATION

- If you are a provider, take a moment to pull up your marketing materials. Does your brochure use language that is inclusive and welcoming to transgender and gender-expansive clients? Does your website unintentionally reinforce the gender binary? Do you notice any potential red flags? What changes would represent your services as more inclusive of transgender clients?

- Imagine you have a gender-expansive client who has experienced difficulty finding treatment for eating disorders at a higher level of care. How can you help this client to determine if the recommended program is welcoming and inclusive? Jot down specific questions that you can ask the intake counselor or marketing representative to assist your client in this process.

- Do an online search for training programs that may complement your client knowledge of eating disorders and/or trans-affirmative counseling. What opportunities are available to you? How would sign up for such training help in your professional development?

Appendix 1: Summary of Guidelines for Clinicians

1. Foster an environment in which clients feel respected in the uniqueness of their gender identities.

2. Seek out training on eating disorders, body image, and gender diversity (as needed).

3. Create intentional safe space so that gender-diverse clients feel welcomed and valued

4. Value body diversity and expression.

5. Communicate understanding of gender expansiveness through use of language.

6. Reject the gender binary; understand that gender is multi-dimensional.

7. Recognize that gender identity can develop on many different trajectories—cisgender, gender diverse, and transgender—and that all are normal developmental paths.

8. Affirm identity: intentionally use language that aligns with the person's gender identity.

9. Provide clients with space and reassurance to take their own gender journeys. Do so without an outcome in mind, whether this outcome is supportive or counter to trans identity.

10. Accept the reality of gender-based minority stress and provide support in navigating this.

11. Understand the medical aspects of eating disorders and transition. While you do not have to be an expert, this understanding is important in your work.

12. Be comfortable in discussing coming out and transition.

13. Accept that surgeries and other ways of affirming gender may be necessary for full body acceptance.

14. Partner with sources of support, such as eating disorders and trans health organizations.

15. When referring for services, assess whether programs honor diversity in body size and presentation.

16. Be able to advocate for clients when needed.

17. Recognize your own gender and body privilege.

Appendix 2: Resource Guide

This guide includes a partial list of resources for healthcare providers working with transgender and gender-expansive clients. Descriptions of each resource are based on information from the resource's website and do not imply endorsement.

National resources

American Psychological Association, Office on Sexual Orientation and Gender Diversity

This office seeks to apply knowledge of gender identity and sexual orientation to psychological practice. The website contains guidelines and resources.

www.apa.org/pi/lgbt

FTM (Female to Male) International

Offers resources and support groups for transgender males and their families domestically and internationally.

www.ftmi.org

GLBTQ Legal Advocates & Defenders (GLAD)

Provides online resources about LGBTQ and HIV rights. GLAD is a non-profit legal rights organization that works to end discrimination based on sexual orientation, HIV status, and gender identity and expression.

www.glad.org

Gay and Lesbian Alliance Against Defamation (GLAAD)

Works through media outlets to promote acceptance from the LGBTQ community.

www.glaad.org

Gay, Lesbian, and Straight Education Network (GLSEN)

An education organization focused on LGBTQ rights within school environments (bullying, harassment, etc.).

www.glsen.org

Gender Spectrum

Educates the public to promote better understanding of gender and gender diversity.

www.genderspectrum.org

Human Rights Campaign

Civil rights organization that advocates for LGBTQ equality and educates the public about LGBTQ issues.

www.hrc.org

National Association of Social Workers (NASW), LGBT Issues

Practice organization within the NASW that provides tools, information, and resources to enhance social workers' capacity to support the LGBTQ+ community.

www.socialworkers.org/Practice/LGBT

National Center for Transgender Equality

Advocates for political change and works to increase understanding and acceptance of transgender people.

https://transequality.org

National LGBTQ Task Force

A social justice advocacy group that trains activists to support LGBTQ rights in areas including housing, employment, healthcare, and retirement.

www.thetaskforce.org

Parents, Families and Friends of Lesbians and Gays (PFLAG)

A parent support group that provides parent/family support and promotes allyship for LGBTQ people.

www.pflag.org

Transgender American Veterans Association (TAVA)

An advocacy group for transgender veterans from the US military that ensures these veterans receive appropriate care for medical and mental health conditions.

http://transveteran.org

Transgender Law and Policy Institute (TLPI)

Organization that engages in advocacy for transgender people, particularly in the areas of law and policy.

www.transgenderlaw.org

Transgender Legal Defense & Education Fund (TLDEF)

Civil rights organization that focuses on transgender equality.

www.transgenderlegal.org

Trans Student Educational Resources

Youth-led organization focused on rights of trans and gender-nonconforming students through advocacy and empowerment. This is the creator of the Gender Unicorn.

www.transstudent.org/gender

Trans Youth Equality Foundation

Provides education, advocacy, and support for transgender children, youth, and their families.

www.transyouthequality.org

Trans Youth Family Allies (TYFA)

Family and youth empowerment organization that partners with educators, service providers, and communities. A key area of focus is suicide and violence prevention.

www.imatyfa.org

The Trevor Project

Provides crisis intervention and suicide prevention services to lesbian, gay, bisexual, transgender, queer, and questioning young people under the age of 25. It also operates the Trevor Lifeline, a confidential service that offers trained counselors.

www.thetrevorproject.org

World Professional Association for Transgender Health (WPATH)

WPATH promotes evidence-based care, education, research, advocacy, and public policy with respect to transgender health. WPATH also publishes standards of care for the trans community.

www.wpath.org

Regional resources
Northeast

Allentown Women's Center (Bethlehem, PA)

Services include hormone replacement therapy, assistance with legal document changes, upper/lower exams, self-injection instruction, referrals, transition care, and abortion care.

www.allentownwomenscenter.com

Bucks LGBTQ Center (Newtown, PA)

Offers psychological care for members of the LGBTQ+ community and their families. Staff also conduct training on issues impacting the LGBTQ community.

https://buckslgbtq.com

Callen-Lorde Community Health Center (New York, NY)

Offers trans-affirmative healthcare services on a sliding scale. Advocates for LGBTQ health issues.

http://callen-lorde.org

Chase Brexton (Baltimore, MD)

The LGBTQ Health Resource Center within Chase Brexton connects members of the LGBTQ community with services and resources.

www.chasebrexton.org

Community Healthcare Network NYC (Bronx, NY)

Provides community-based primary care, mental health and social services for diverse populations in underserved communities throughout New York City.

www.chnnyc.org

Dartmouth-Hitchcock Medical Center Transgender Clinic (Lebanon, NH)

Offers healthcare to patients seeking hormonal and/or surgical reassignment of gender.

www.dartmouth-hitchcock.org/endo/transgender_clinic.html

Evergreen Health Services (Buffalo, NY)

Provides medical, pharmacy, housing, mental health, nutrition, transportation and syringe-exchange services for people who are underserved by the healthcare system, including trans people.

http://evergreenhs.org

Fenway Health Transgender Program (Boston, MA)

Offers healthcare, education, research, and advocacy for members of the LGBTQ+ community, as well as professional training programs (many available online).

https://fenwayhealth.org/care/medical/transgender-health

Gender and Sexuality Development Clinic at Children's Hospital of Philadelphia (Philadelphia, PA)

Offers psychosocial and medical support for gender variant, gender-expansive, and transgender children and youth up to the age of 21, and their families.

www.chop.edu/centers-programs/gender-and-sexuality-development-clinic/our-team

Mazzoni Center (Philadelphia, PA)

Offers healthcare, counseling services, HIV prevention and care, and legal services for members of the LGBTQ+ community.

www.mazzonicenter.org

Ryan Health (New York, NY)

Provides primary care, behavioral health services, and HIV prevention and care. Offers services regardless of the ability to pay.

https://ryanhealth.org

South

Health Brigade (Richmond, VA)

Provides health services, including hormone treatment, medication assistance, psychiatric referrals, voice therapy, support groups, and legal services.

www.healthbrigade.org

Magic City Wellness Center (Birmingham, AL)

Offers services including hormone replacement therapy, counseling, testing for HIV and sexually transmitted diseases, and support groups.

www.magiccitywellnesscenter.org

Trans Health Initiative (Atlanta, GA)

Provides sensitive, safe, and affordable healthcare to transgender, gender-nonconforming and intersex clients from across the South. Services for trans men include hormone therapy, wellness exams, lower exams, chest exams, and gender-marker letter changes. Services for trans women, nonbinary, and intersex clients include testing for HIV and sexually transmitted diseases, wellness lab work, chest exams, and gender-marker letter changes.

www.feministcenter.org/trans-health-initiative

Whitman-Walker Health (Washington, DC)

Provides services such as hormone therapy, testing for HIV and sexually transmitted diseases, gynecology, group psychotherapy, individual psychotherapy, peer support services, and legal services.

www.whitman-walker.org

YES Institute (Miami, FL)

Suicide prevention through education on gender and orientation.

https://yesinstitute.org

Midwest

Chicago Women's Health Center (Chicago, IL)

The center's Trans Greater Access Project focuses on increasing access to health services for trans-identified individuals. Services include primary care, hormone therapy, counseling and therapy, alternative insemination, and gynecological services.

www.chicagowomenshealthcenter.org

Howard Brown Health Center (Chicago, IL)

Runs programs that address the needs of trans and gender-nonconforming clients, as well as medical, behavioral health, and case management.

https://howardbrown.org

KC Care Health Center (Kansas City, MO)

Provides affordable, integrated health services, including HIV education and testing, hormone therapy, and psychiatric counseling.

https://kccare.org

Transgender Health Clinic at Cincinnati Children's Hospital (Cincinnati, OH)

Offers services for patients aged 5–24 years old: medical and psychosocial support, treatment planning, and service referral.

www.cincinnatichildrens.org/service/a/adolescent-medicine/programs/transgender

Transgender Health Services at University of Minnesota Medical School (Minneapolis, MN)

Individual, group, and family psychotherapy, psychiatric services, specialty medical care, hormone therapy, consultation and advocacy about gender issues, and referrals for surgical interventions. Services are inclusive to gender-creative children as well as transgender and gender-nonconforming adolescents and adults.

www.sexualhealth.umn.edu/clinic-center-sexual-health/transgender-health-services

West

API Wellness Clinic (San Francisco, CA)

An LGBTQ and people-of-color health organization that works to create safe spaces, events, and services for the trans community. Services offered include case management and medical services, mental health and substance use support, and social groups, and special events. The clinic serves trans people of color, trans people living with HIV, homeless trans people, transgender youth, and anyone on the trans spectrum.

https://sfcommunityhealth.org

Boulder Valley Women's Health Center (Boulder, CO)

Provides a wide variety of reproductive and sexual healthcare services for people of all genders, including birth control, annual exams, testing for sexually transmitted infections, transgender hormone therapy, a teen clinic, and more. The center offers comprehensive sexual and gender-affirming health services for individuals of all gender and sexual identities.

www.boulderwomenshealth.org

Equality Arizona (Statewide)

Provides support groups, advocacy, community education, and training for businesses, service providers, community members, and allies.

http://equalityarizona.org

Gay and Lesbian Community Center of Southern Nevada, The (Las Vegas, NV)

A community-based organization that supports the queer community, its allies, and low to moderate income residents in Southern Nevada. The center provides transgender and non-conforming individuals a safe place to relate to peers, seek guidance, exchange clothing, and expand social networks.

http://thecenterlv.org

Gender Health Center (Sacramento, CA)

Provides accessible therapy and counseling for the gender diverse community.

www.thegenderhealthcenter.org

Gender Pathways Clinic (San Francisco, CA)

Provides care for transgender and gender-expansive patients. A specialist team consists of providers from internal medicine, gynecology, psychiatry, surgery and nursing that provide gender-affirming hormone therapy, sexual and reproductive healthcare, mental health services, and surgical evaluations and procedures.

https://thrive.kaiserpermanente.org/care-near-you/northern-california/sanfrancisco/departments/gender-pathways-clinic

Lavender Clinic (Honolulu, HI)

Provides healthcare, leadership, programs, education, and services for the transgender, lesbian, gay, bisexual, queer, and intersex communities. Services include speech and voice training, transgender services, hormone therapy, and HIV prevention therapy.

https://lavendercenterandclinic.org

Los Angeles LGBT Center (Los Angeles, CA)

Supports transgender and transitioning people with employment, healthcare, legal assistance, housing, advocacy, and education.

https://lalgbtcenter.org

Lyon-Martin Health Services (San Francisco, CA)

Provides healthcare for heterosexual women, bisexual women, lesbians and transgender people. Transgender health services include trans-affirmative gynecologic care, hormone therapy for gender transition, testing for HIV and sexually transmitted diseases, mental health counseling, and referrals for gender-affirming surgery.

http://lyon-martin.org

Southern Arizona Gender Alliance (SAGA)

Supports and advocates for Southern Arizona's community of trans identities: transsexual, transgender, genderqueer, masculine of center, feminine of center, non-binary, two-spirit, butch, femme, gender fluid, and intersex. SAGA offers various support, social and discussion groups that reflect aspects of gender and society.

https://sagatucson.org/wp

Tom Waddell Clinic (San Francisco, CA)

Serves adults experiencing homelessness, residents of supportive housing, and other members of San Francisco's Tenderloin neighborhood. Services include comprehensive HIV prevention and care; Hepatitis C treatment; office-based opioid treatment; transgender care; integrated behavioral health services; podiatry and dental services.

www.twtransgenderclinic.org

Trans Spectrum of Arizona (Phoenix, AZ)

Provides service, support, and a social outlet for transgender and gender-nonconforming individuals and their allies.

https://tsaz.org

Transgender Resource Center of New Mexico (Albuquerque, NM)

Provides support, community, and connection to transgender, gender-nonconforming, nonbinary, and gender-diverse people and their families through advocacy, education, and direct services. Offers several different support groups and a Food Justice Project that addresses issues of food insecurity and chronic hunger in the trans community.

www.tgrcnm.org

UCSF Transgender Care Navigation Program (San Francisco, CA)

Provides services like hormone therapy, gender-affirming surgery, voice and speech therapy, legal name and gender change, and sexual health.

https://transcare.ucsf.edu

Appendix 3: Glossary

Agender: A term for people who do not identify themselves as having a particular gender. They may also identify as *genderqueer* or *nonbinary*.

Alexithymia: Without words for emotions.

Assigned sex: Classification of people as male or female at birth, usually based on the body/genitalia. Also known as *natal sex*.

Binding: Flattening the breasts using constrictive materials. Commercially available binders are the safest method of binding and should not be worn for more than 8–12 hours.

Bisexual: Sexual attraction or sexual behavior toward both males and females.

Body dissatisfaction: Feelings of discontent about the body, often resulting from the difference between an individual's actual body size or shape and the person's own ideal size or shape.

Body-image distortion: A state in which the person's perception of the body is inaccurate.

Bottom surgery: A surgery process that allows correction of body incongruence; the goal of transfeminine bottom surgery is to transform the male genitalia and reconstruct it into that of a female; the goal of transmasculine bottom surgery is to transform the female genitalia and reconstruct it into that of a male.

Butch: Lesbian whose appearance and behavior are more traditionally masculine.

Cisgender: Person whose gender identity and perception of body aligns to their assigned sex.

Closeted: An individual who chooses not to disclose an LGBT identity for personal or social reasons.

Coming out: Self-disclosure of gender identity or sexual orientation.

Cross-dresser: A person who, in specific situations, displays a gender expression that is usually reserved for another gender. Some people cross-dress as part of gender performance associated with drag queens and drag kings.

Detransition: The process of changing one's gender presentation and/or sex characteristics back to one's assigned sex after an earlier transgender transition. Also called *retransition*.

Dead name: A person's birth name prior to social transition.

Dissociation: A trauma response in which the person detaches from a physical and/or emotional experience.

Ectomorphic: A slender body build with slight muscular development.

Endomorphic: A slightly wide body build, with a thick rib cage, wide hips, and shorter limbs.

Experiential therapies: Therapeutic technique that uses expressive tools and activities (arts, music, guided imagery writing) to process emotional situations within a safe, contained environment.

Gatekeeping: Any requirement that controls or accesses services available to transgender people. This is often used in regard to medical transition, and is an alternative to the *informed consent model*.

Gay: Sexually attracted solely to people of the same sex.

Gender: A cognitive construct. The internal state of being "male" or "female," as defined by social and cultural expectations rather than biological factors.

Gender dysphoria: Conflict between a person's physical or assigned gender and discomfort with the body or feeling of being in the "wrong" body.

Gender expression: The ways in which people externally communicate gender identity to others (e.g., feminine, masculine, butch, androgynous, femme).

Gender fluid: The experience in which a person's internal sense of gender varies. At different times, the person may identify as identify as male, female, neutral, a nonbinary identity, or a combination of identities.

Gender identity: A person's internal sense of being male, female, both, neither, or other gender(s).

Gender journey: The process of exploring gender identity.

Gender marker: The legal indicator on birth certificates, driver's licenses, passports, and other forms of government identification that indicate male ("M") or female ("F").

Gender nonbinary/gender nonconforming: Expressing oneself in ways that are not consistent with the societal norms for one's assigned sex.

Genderqueer: An umbrella term that encompasses many types of queer identities. Genderqueer has been used as an adjective to refer to people who do not adhere to distinctions of gender, regardless of their self-defined gender identity.

Informed consent model: In the context of physical transition, the idea that the client's knowledge of the risks and benefits of surgery is all that should be required to obtain hormones and surgical procedures. This is an alternative to *gatekeeping*.

Intersectionality: The interconnected nature of social categorizations, such as race, class, and gender. These categorizations may apply to an individual or group and create overlapping systems of discrimination.

Interoception: Understanding and feeling what's going on inside the body, including cues related to hunger, fullness, temperature, or thirst.

Intuitive eating: An approach to working with disordered eating that addresses the effects of chronic dieting by promoting an attitude of body acceptance, honoring body cues of hunger and fullness, healthy exercise, and varied eating choices.

Lesbian: Woman who is romantically or sexually attracted solely to other women.

LGBTQ+: Acronym for lesbian, gay, bisexual, transgender, queer and all others within the overall *queer* community, based on one's gender identity and sexual or romantic orientation.

Microaggression: Everyday verbal, nonverbal, and environmental slight, usually unintentional, that communicates derogatory or negative messages.

Microassault: Form of microaggression involving purposeful discriminatory action, such as a verbal attack or avoidant behavior.

Minority stress: Chronically high levels of stress in members of stigmatized minority groups, often stemming from interpersonal prejudice and discrimination.

Misgendering: Referring to someone using a word, especially a pronoun or form of address, that does not correctly reflect the gender with which the person identifies.

Narrative therapy: Form of therapy that that seeks to help people identify their values and the skills and knowledge they have to live these values so that they can effectively confront problems.

Natal sex: See *assigned sex.*

Nonbinary, nonbinary gender: Any gender identity that does not fit the male and female binary. Also known as *genderqueer.*

Out: As a verb, to disclose someone's gender identity without the person's consent.

Packing: Wearing padding or a phallic object to create the appearance of having a penis and male bulge. Many trans males feel more comfortable and are able to *pass* by packing.

Pansexual: Not limited in sexual choice with regard to biological sex, gender, or gender identity.

Paraphilia: Condition in which a person's sexual arousal and gratification depend on fantasizing about and engaging in unorthodox sexual behavior.

Pass: A person's ability to be regarded at a glance as either a cisgender man or woman.

Primary sex characteristics: Body structures directly concerned with reproduction, such as the testes, ovaries, and external genitalia.

Queer: An umbrella term for sexual and gender minorities who are not heterosexual and/or not cisgender.

Questioning: The questioning of one's own gender, sexual identity, or sexual orientation; the process of exploration by people who may be unsure, still exploring, or concerned about applying a social label to themselves.

Retransition: See *detransition.*

Sex: A biological construct based on the male/female binary.

Sexual orientation: An enduring emotional, romantic, sexual, affectional, and relational attraction to other people, determined by the personally significant or romantic attractions one has and the way in which someone identifies.

Schemas: Beliefs, experiences, and generalizations about the body and self.

Secondary sex characteristics: Biological characteristics that externally distinguish a male from a female and are not directly concerned with reproduction. Examples include breast development, voice pitch, facial hair, and body shape.

Social transition: A process that occurs when a person makes changes in appearance or presentation in social situations to reflect gender identity. It may include telling others about gender or changing one's name.

Stealth: A person's ability to *pass* as the dominant identity (cisgender male or female, heterosexual, etc.) and living under the assumption of this identity rather than being connected to the marginalized identity (e.g., transgender male or female, gender nonbinary, lesbian, gay).

Top surgery: A surgery process that allows correction of body incongruence; for transfeminine people, this may involve breast augmentation; for transmasculine people, it may involve bilateral mastectomy and male chest reconstruction.

Transfeminine: Describes transgender people assigned male at birth, but who identify with femininity to a greater extent than masculinity.

Transgender/trans: An umbrella term for people whose gender identity differs from the sex they were assigned at birth. People who are transgender often express the feeling of having been born in the "wrong" body.

Transition: Process of developing and assuming a gender expression that corresponds with gender identity. Transition may involve changes to the body, such as hormones or binding, or non-body-related changes, such use of preferred name.

Transmasculine: Describes transgender people assigned female at birth, but who identify with masculinity to a greater extent than femininity.

Transphobia: The fear or, hatred of, and discrimination against, individuals who are transgender or gender nonbinary.

Transvestite: Sometimes used to describe a person who cross-dresses, though this term has negative connotations and is discouraged from any clinical conversation unless the client uses the term first in self-identification.

Two-spirit: Term used by certain indigenous peoples to signify a third gender (nonconforming or variant).

WPATH: Acronym for the World Professional Association for Transgender Health. Author of the current standards of care guidelines for professionals working with transgender and gender-nonconforming clients or patients.

References

Ålgars, M., Santtila, P., & Sandnabba, N.K. (2010). "Conflicted gender identity, body dissatisfaction, and disordered eating in adult men and women." *Sex Roles*, 63, 118–125

American Psychiatric Association (2013). *Diagnostic and Statistical Manual of Mental Disorders* (fifth edition). Washington, DC: APA.

American Psychological Association (2016). *Ethical Principles of Psychologists and Code of Conduct*. Retrieved February 11, 2018, from www.apa.org/ethics/code.

American Psychological Association (2015). *Guidelines for Psychological Practice With Transgender and Gender Nonconforming People*. Retrieved February 25, 2018 from www.apa.org/practice/guidelines/transgender.pdf.

Anderson-Fye, E.P. (2011). "Body images in Non-Western Cultures." In T.F. Cash & L. Smolak (eds) *Body Image: A Handbook of Science and Prevention* (pp.244–252). New York, NY: The Guilford Press.

Arizona Board of Regents (1997). Eating issues and body image continuum. Retrieved January 10, 2019 from www.health.arizona.edu/sites/default/files/continuum2.pdf.

Austin, A. & Craig, S. (2015). "Transgender affirmative cognitive behavioral therapy: Clinical considerations and applications." *Professional Psychology: Research and Practice*, 46(1), 21–29.

Austin, A., Craig S.L., & Alessi, E.J. (2017). "Affirmative Cognitive Behavior Therapy with Transgender and Gender Nonconforming Adults." *Psychiatric Clinics in North America*, 40(1), 141–156.

Austin, A., Craig, S., & D'Souza, S. (2017). "An AFFIRMative cognitive behavioral intervention for transgender youth: Preliminary effectiveness." *Professional Psychology: Research and Practice*. 1–8. Retrieved from: http://dx.doi.org/10.1037/pro0000154.

Awad, G.H., Norwood, C., Taylor, D.S., Martinez, M., *et al.* (2015). "Beauty and body image concerns among African American college women." *The Journal of Black Psychology*, 41(6), 540–564.

Baker, L. & Gringart, E. (2009). "Body image and self-esteem in older adulthood." *Ageing and Society*, 29(06), 977–995.

Baum, B., Brill, S., Brown, J., Delpercio, A., *et al.* (2012). *Supporting and Caring for Our Transgender Youth*. Retrieved January 21, 2018 from http://assets2.hrc.org/files/assets/resources/Gender-expansive-youth-report-final.pdf.

Bem, S.L. (1981). "Gender schema theory: A cognitive account of sex typing." *Psychological Review*, 88, 354–364.

Benenson, J.F., Markovits, H., Thompson, M.E., & Wrangham, R.W. (2011). "Under threat of social exclusion, females exclude more than males." *Psychological Science*, 22, 538–544.

Bockting, W. & Coleman, E. (2007). "Developmental Stages of the Transgender Coming-Out Process." In R. Ettner, S. Monstrey, & A. Eyler (eds) *Principles of Transgender Medicine and Surgery* (pp.185–208). New York, NY: Haworth.

Bockting, W., Coleman, E., Deutsch, M.B., Guillamon, A., *et al.* (2016). "Adult development and quality of life of transgender and gender nonconforming people." *Current Opinion in Endocrinology, Diabetes, and Obesity*, 23(2), 188–197.

Bockting, W.O., Miner, M.H., Swinburne Romine, R.E., Hamilton, A., & Coleman, E. (2013). "Stigma, mental health, and resilience in an online sample of the US transgender population." *American Journal of Public Health*, 103(5), 943–951.

Bornstein, K. (2013). *My New Gender Workbook: A Step-by-Step Guide to Achieving World Peace through Gender Anarchy and Sex Positivity*. New York, NY: Routledge.

Bungener, S.L., Steensma, T.D., Cohen-Kettenis, P.T., & de Vries, A.L. (2017). "Sexual and romantic experiences of transgender youth before gender-affirmative treatment." *Pediatrics*, 139 (3):e20162283.

Brayboy, D. (2017). *Two Spirits, One Heart, Five Genders*. Indian Country Today. Retrieved July 8, 2019 from https://newsmaven.io/indiancountrytoday/archive/two-spirits-one-heart-five-genders-9UH_xnbfVEWQHWkjNn0rQQ.

Calzo, J.P., Blashill, A.J., Brown, T.A., & Argenal, R.L. (2017). "Eating disorders and disordered weight and shape control behaviors in sexual minority populations." *Current Psychiatry Reports*, 19(8), 49.

Cash, T.F. (2011). "Cognitive Behavioral Perspectives on Body Image." In T.F. Cash & L. Smolak (eds) *Body Image: A Handbook of Science and Prevention* (pp.39–47). New York, NY: The Guilford Press.

Cash, T.F., Maikkula, C.L., & Yamamiya, Y. (2004). "Baring the body in the bedroom: Body image, sexual self-schemas, and sexual functioning among college women and men." *Electronic Journal of Human Sexuality*, 7, 1–9.

Cavanaugh, T., Hopwood, R., & Lambert, C. (2016). "Informed consent in the medical care of transgender and gender-nonconforming patient." *AMA Journal of Ethics*, 18(11),1147–1155. Retrieved July 8, 2019 from https://journalofethics.ama-assn.org/article/informed-consent-medical-care-transgender-and-gender-nonconforming-patients/2016-11.

Clements-Nolle, K., Marx, R., & Katz, M. (2006). "Attempted suicide among transgender persons: The influence of gender-based discrimination and victimization." *Journal of Homosexuality*, 51(3), 53–69.

Coleman, E., Bockting, W., Botzer, M., Cohen-Kettenis, P., *et al.* (2012). "Standards of care for the health of transsexual, transgender, and gender-nonconforming people, Version 7." *International Journal of Transgenderism*, 13(4), 165–232. Retrieved July 8, 2019 from www.wpath.org/media/cms/Documents/SOC%20v7/Standards%20of%20Care_V7%20Full%20 Book_English.pdf.

Crooks, R. & Baur, K. (2017). *Our Sexuality* (13th edition). Belmont, CA: Wadsworth.

Crow, S.J., Swanson, S.A., Peterson, C.B., Crosby, R.D., Wonderlich, S.A., & Mitchell, J.E. (2012). "Latent class analysis of eating disorders: Relationship to mortality." *Journal of Abnormal Psychology*, 121, 225–231.

Davinson, T.E. & McCabe, M.P. (2005). "Relationships between men's and women's body image and their psychological, social, and sexual functioning." *Sex Roles*, 52, 463–475.

de Vries, A.L., McGuire, J.K., Steensma, T.D., Wagenaar, E.C., Doreleijers, T.A., & Cohen-Kettenis, P.T. (2014). "Young adult psychological outcome after puberty suppression and gender reassignment." *Pediatrics*, 134, 696–704.

Diemer, E.W., White Hughto, J.M., Gordon, A.R., Guss, C., Austin, S.B., & Randysner, S.L. (2018). "Beyond the binary: Differences in eating disorder prevalence by gender identity in a transgender sample." *Transgender Health*, 3(1), 17–23.

Donaghue, N. (2009). "Body satisfaction, sexual self-schemas and subjective well-being in women." *Body Image*, 6(1), 37–42.

Duffy, M.E., Henkel, K.E., & Earnshaw, V.A. (2016). "Transgender clients' experiences of eating disorder treatment." *Journal of LGBT Issues in Counseling*, 10(3), 136–149.

El-Hadi, H., Stone, J., & Temple-Oberle, C., Harrop A.R. (2018). "Gender-affirming surgery for transgender individuals: Perceived satisfaction and barriers to care." *Plastic Surgery*, 26(4), 263–268.

Erikson, E.H. (1968). *Identity, Youth and Crisis*. New York, NY: W.W. Norton & Company.

Finn, C. (2011). *Please Hear What I'm Not Saying: A Poem's Reach Around the World*. Bloomington, IN: AuthorHouse.

Franko, D.L. & Roehrig, J.P. (2011). "African American Body Images." In T.F. Cash & L. Smolak (eds) *Body Image: A Handbook of Science and Prevention* (pp.221–228). New York, NY: The Guilford Press.

Giles, J.W. & Heyman, G.D. (2005). "Young children's beliefs about the relationship between gender and aggressive behavior." *Child Development*, 76(1), 107–121.

Gladden, R.M., Vivolo-Kantor, A.M., Hamburger, M.E., & Lumpkin, C.D. (2013). *Bullying Surveillance Among Youths: Uniform Definitions for Public Health and Recommended Data Elements, Version 1.0.* Atlanta, GA: National Center for Injury Prevention and Control, Centers for Disease Control and Prevention and US Department of Education.

Gordon, A., Austin, B.S., Krieger, N., White Hughto, J.M., & Reisner, S.L. (2016). "'I have to constantly prove to myself, to people, that I fit the bill': Perspectives on weight and shape control behaviors among low-income, ethnically diverse young transgender women." *Social Science Medicine*, 165, 141–149.

Grant, J.M., Mottet, L., Tanis, J., Harrison, J., Herman, J.L., & Keisling, M. (2011). *Injustice at Every Turn: A Report of the National Transgender Discrimination Survey.* Washington, DC: National Center for Transgender Equality and National Gay and Lesbian Task Force.

Grossman, A.H. & D'Augelli, A.R. (2006). "Transgender youth: Invisible and vulnerable." Co-published simultaneously in *Journal of Homosexuality* (Harrington Park Press, an imprint of The Haworth Press) Vol. 51, No. 1, 111–128; and in J.Harcourt (ed.) *Current Issues in Lesbian, Gay, Bisexual, and Transgender Health.* New York, NY: Harrington Park Press, an imprint of The Haworth Press, pp.111–128.

Guss, C.E., Williams, D.N., Reisner, S.L., Austin, S.B., & Katz-Wise, S.L. (2016). "Disordered weight management behaviors and non-prescription steroid use in Massachusetts transgender youth." *Journal of Adolescent Health*, 58, S102–S103.

Haas, A.P., Rogers, P.L., & Herman, J. (2014). Suicide attempts among transgender and gender non-conforming adults. Retrieved January 19, 2018 from https://williamsinstitute.law.ucla.edu/wp-content/uploads/AFSP-Williams-Suicide-Report-Final.pdf.

Harrison, S., Rowlinson, M., & Hill, A.J. (2016). "'No fat friend of mine': Young children's responses to overweight and disability." *Body Image*, 18, 65–73.

Healthwatch Northamptonshire (2016). Eating disorders and body image: Issues affecting LGBTQ Youth. Retrieved March 18, 2018 from www.healthwatchnorthamptonshire.co.uk/sites/default/files/lgbtq_report_final_oct_2016.pdf.

Hinz, L.D. (2006). *Drawing from Within: Using Art to Treat Eating Disorders.* Philadelphia, PA: Jessica Kingsley Publishers.

Holmes S. (2016). "'Blindness to the obvious?' Treatment experiences and feminist approaches to eating disorders." *Feminism & Psychology*, 26, 464–486.

Human Rights Campaign (n.d.). *Sexual Orientation and Gender Identity Definitions.* Retrieved April 10, 2018 from www.hrc.org/resources/sexual-orientation-and-gender-identity-terminology-and-definitions.

Huxley, C.J., Halliwell, E., & Clarke, V. (2015). "An examination of the Tripartite Influence Model of body image: Does women's sexual identity make a difference?" *Psychology of Women Quarterly*, 39(3), 337–348.

James, S.E., Herman, J.L., Rankin, S., Keisling, M., Mottet, L., & Anafi, M. (2016). *The Report of the 2015 U.S. Transgender Survey.* Washington, DC: National Center for Transgender Equality.

Janicka, A. & Forcier, M. (2016). "Transgender and gender nonconforming youth: Psychosocial and medical considerations." *Rhode Island Medical Journal.* Retrieved March 10, 2018 from www.rimed.org/rimedicaljournal/2016/09/2016-09-31-adolescent-janicka.pdf.

Klein, C. & Gorzalka, B.B. (2009). "Sexual functioning in transsexuals following hormone therapy and genital surgery: A review (CME)." *Journal of Sexual Medicine*, 6(11), 2922–2939.

Klimek, P., Murray, S.B., Brown, T., Gonzales, I., & Blashill, A.J. (2018). "Thinness and muscularity internalization: Associations with disordered eating and muscle dysmorphia in men." *International Journal of Eating Disorders*, 51(4), 352–357.

Kohlberg, L. (1966). "A Cognitive-Developmental Analysis of Children's Sex-Role Concepts and Attitudes." In E.E. Maccody (ed.) *The Development of Sex Differences.* Stanford, CA: Stanford University Press.

Kohlberg, L. (1969). "Stage and Sequence: The Cognitive-Developmental Approach to Socialization." In D.A. Goslin (ed.) *Handbook of Socialization Theory and Research*. Chicago, IL: Rand McNally.

Kosciw, J.G., Greytak, E.A., Diaz, E.M., & Bartkiewicz, M.J. (2010). *The 2009 National School Climate Survey: The experiences of lesbian, gay, bisexual and transgender youth in our nation's schools*. New York, NY: Gay, Lesbian and Straight Education Network (GLSEN).

Lavender, J.M., Brown, T.A., & Murray, S.B. (2017). "Men, muscles, and eating disorders: An overview of traditional and muscularity-oriented disordered eating." *Current Psychiatry Reports*, 19(6), 32.

Lev, A. (2004). *Transgender Emergence: Understanding Diverse Gender Identities and Expressions*. Retrieved May 1, 2018 from www.choicesconsulting.com/assets/pro_writing/transgender%5B1%5D.pdf.

Lev, A.I. & Alie, L. (2012). "Transgender and Gender Nonconforming Children and Youth: Developing Culturally Competent Systems of Care." In S.K. Fisher, J. Poirier, & G.M. Blau (eds) *Improving Emotional and Behavioral Outcomes for LGBT Youth: A Guide for Professionals*. Baltimore, MD: Brookes Publishing Company.

Levine, P. (2008). *Healing Trauma*. Boulder, CO: Sounds True.

Levine, P. (2012). *In An Unspoken Voice: How the Body Releases Trauma and Restores Goodness*. New York, NY: Penguin Random House Books.

Lorber, J. & Moore, L.J. (2011). *Gendered Bodies: Feminist Perspectives*. New York, NY: Oxford University Press.

Martin, C.L. & Ruble, D.N. (2010). "Patterns of gender development." *Annual Review of Psychology*, 61, 353–381.

Marzullo, M.A. & Libman, A.J. (2009). *Hate Crimes and Violence Against LGBT People*. Washington, DC: Human Rights Campaign.

McBride, S. (2018). *Tomorrow Will Be Different*. New York, NY: Crown Type Archetype.

McConnell, E.A., Birkett, M., & Mustanski, B. (2016). "Families matter: Social support and mental health trajectories among lesbian, gay, bisexual, and transgender youth." *Journal of Adolescent Health*, 5, 674–680.

McCarthy, M.M., Auger, A.P., & Bale, T.L. (2009). "The epigenetics of sex differences in the brain." *Journal of Neuroscience*, 29(41), 12815–12823.

McGuire, J.K., Anderson, C.R., Toomey, R.B., & Russell, S.T. (2010). "School climate for transgender youth: A mixed method investigation of student experiences and school responses." *Journal of Youth and Adolescence*, 39(10), 1175–1188.

McKay, T., Lindquist, C., & Misra, S. (2017). "Understanding (and acting on) 20 years of research on violence and LGBTQ+ communities." *Trauma, Violence and Abuse*, Jan 1:1524838017728708. doi: 10.1177/1524838017728708.

McLean, S., Paxton, S.J., & Wertheim, E.H. (2010). "Factors associated with body dissatisfaction and disordered eating in women in midlife." *International Journal of Eating Disorders*, 43, 527–536.

Meyer, I.H. (1995). "Minority stress and mental health in gay men." *Journal of Health and Social Behavior*, 36, 38–56.

Meyer, I.H. (2003). "Prejudice, social stress, and mental health in lesbian, gay, and bisexual populations: Conceptual issues and research evidence." *Psychological Bulletin*, 129, 674–697.

Murnen, S.K. (2011). "Gender and Body Images." In T.F. Cash & L. Smolak (eds) *Body Image: A Handbook of Science and Prevention* (pp.173–179). New York, NY: The Guilford Press.

National Association of Social Workers. (2017). Code of ethics of the National Association of Social Workers. Retrieved February 11, 2018, from www.socialworkers.org/About/Ethics/Code-of-Ethics/Code-of-Ethics-English.

National Center for Transgender Equality (2016) *Supporting the Transgender People in Your Life: A Guide to Being a Good Ally*. Retrieved March 7, 2018 from https://transequality.org/issues/resources/supporting-the-transgender-people-in-your-life-a-guide-to-being-a-good-ally.

Nawaz, S. (2011). "The relationship of parental and peer attachment bonds with the identity development during adolescence." *Journal of Social Sciences*, 5, 104–119.

Nicholls, D.E., Lynn, R., & Viner, R.M. (2011). "Childhood eating disorders: British national surveillance study." *British Journal of Psychiatry*, 198, 295–301.

Nuttbrock, L., Bockting, W., Rosenblum, A., Hwahng, S., *et al.* (2014). "Gender abuse and major depression among transgender women: A prospective study of vulnerability and resilience." *American Journal of Public Health*, 104(11), 2191–2198.

Ogden, P. & Fisher, J. (2015). *Sensorimotor Psychotherapy*. New York, NY: W.W. Norton & Company.

Pepper, R. (ed.) (2012). *Transitions of the Heart*. Jersey City, NJ: Cleis Press.

Pleak, R.R. (2009). "Formation of transgender identities in adolescence." *Journal of Gay & Lesbian Mental Health*, 13, 282–291.

Pont, S., Puhl, R., Cook, S., & Slusser, W. (2017). "Stigma experienced by children and adolescents with obesity." *Pediatrics*, 140(6).

Poppe, I., Simons, A., Glazemakers, I., & Van West, D. (2015). "Early-onset eating disorders: A review of the literature." *Tijdschrift voor psychiatrie*, 57(11), 805–814.

Price, C.J. & Hooven, C. (2018). "Interoceptive awareness skills for emotion regulation: Theory and approach of Mindful Awareness in Body-Oriented Therapy (MABT)." *Frontiers in Psychology*, 9, 798.

Pujols, Y., Meston, C.M., & Seal, B.N. (2010). "The association between sexual satisfaction and body image in women." *The Journal of Sexual Medicine*, 7 (2 Pt 2), 905–916.

Randysner, S.L., Greytak, E.A., Parsons, J.T., & Ybarra, M.L. (2015). "Gender minority social stress in adolescence: Disparities in adolescent bullying and substance use by gender identity." *Journal of Sex Research,* 52(3), 243–256.

Ricciardelli, L.A. & McCabe, M.P. (2011). "Body Image Development in Adolescent Boys." In T.F. Cash & L. Smolak (eds) *Body Image: A Handbook of Science and Prevention* (pp.85–92). New York, NY: The Guilford Press.

Robinson, K.J., Mountford, V.A., & Sperlinger, D.J. (2013). "Being men with eating disorders: Perspectives of male eating disorder service-users." *Journal of Health Psychology,* 18, 176–186.

Ryan, C. (2009). *Supportive Families, Healthy Children: Helping Families with Lesbian, Gay, Bisexual & Transgender Children*. San Francisco, CA: Family Acceptance Project, Marian Wright Edelman Institute, San Francisco State University.

Ryan, C. & Chen-Hayes, S. (2013). "Educating and Empowering Families of LGBTQ K-12 Students." In E.S. Fisher & K. Komosa-Hawkins (eds) *Creating School Environments to Support Lesbian, Gay, Bisexual, Transgender, and Questioning Students and Families: A Handbook for School Professionals* (pp.209–227). New York, NY: Routledge.

Safer, J.D., Coleman, E., Feldman, J., Garofalo, R., *et al.* (2016). "Barriers to healthcare for transgender individuals." *Current Opinion in Endocrinology, Diabetes, and Obesity*, 23(2), 168–171.

Saleem, F. & Rizvi, S.W. (2017). "Transgender associations and possible etiology: A literature review." *Cureus*, 9(12), e1984.

Sarafrazi N., Hughes, J.P., Borrud, L., Burt, V., & Paulose-Ram, R. (2014). "Perception of weight status in U.S. children and adolescents aged 8–15 years, 2005–2012." *NCHS Data Brief*, (158)1–7.

Schooler, D. & Lowry, L.S. (2011). "Hispanic/Latino Body Images." In T.F. Cash & L. Smolak (eds) *Body Image: A Handbook of Science and Prevention* (pp.237–243). New York, NY: The Guilford Press.

Sevelius, J.M, (2013). "Gender affirmation: A framework for conceptualizing risk behavior among transgender women of color." *Sex Roles*, 68(11–12), 675–689.

Shaffer, D. & Kipp, K. (2013). *Developmental Psychology*. Belmont, CA: Wadsworth.

Smolak, L. (2011). "Body Image Development in Childhood." In T.F. Cash & L. Smolak (eds) *Body Image: A Handbook of Science and Prevention* (pp.67–75). New York, NY: The Guilford Press.

Stolzenberg E.B. & Hughes, B. (2017). "The experiences of incoming transgender college students: New data on gender identity." *Liberal Education*, 103(2). Retrieved March 10, 2018 from www.aacu.org/liberaleducation/2017/spring/stolzenberg_hughes.

Sue, D.W. (2010). *Microaggressions in Everyday Life: Race, Gender, and Sexual Orientation*. Hoboken, NJ: John Wiley & Sons.

Suliman, S., Mkabile, S.G., Fincham, D.S., Ahmed, R., Stein, D.J., & Seedat, S. (2009). "Cumulative effect of multiple trauma on symptoms of posttraumatic stress disorder, anxiety, and depression in adolescents." *Comprehensive Psychiatry*, 50(2), 121–127.

Tandy, K. (2015). *Trans Day of Remembrance is Resilience Above All*. The Establishment. Retrieved July 8, 2019 from https://medium.com/the-establishment/trans-day-of-remembrance-is-resilience-above-all-2e542fd6b147.

Tantleff-Dunn, S. & Linder, D.M. (2011). "Body Image and Social Functioning." In T.F. Cash & L. Smolak (eds) *Body Image: A Handbook of Science and Prevention* (pp.263–270). New York, NY: The Guilford Press.

Testa, R.J., Coolhart, D., & Peta, J. (2015). *The Gender Quest Workbook: A Guide for Teens & Young Adults Exploring Gender Identity*. Oakland, CA: Instant Help Books.

Testa, R.J., Michaels, M., Bliss, W., Rogers, M., Balsam, K., & Joiner, T. (2017). "Suicidal ideation in transgender people: Gender minority stress and interpersonal theory factors." *Journal of Abnormal Psychology*, 126(1), 125–136. doi: 10.1037/abn0000234.

Thapliyal, P., Hay, P., & Conti, J. (2018). "Role of gender in the treatment experiences of people with an eating disorder: A metasynthesis." *Journal of Eating Disorders*, 6, 18. doi:10.1186/s40337-018-0207-1.

Thompson, J.K., Heinberg, L.J., Altabe, M., & Tantleff-Dunn, S. (1999). *Exacting Beauty: Theory, Assessment and Treatment of Body Image Disturbance*. Washington, DC: American Psychological Association.

Thompson, J.K., Shroff, H., Herbozo, S., Cafri, G., Rodriguez, J., & Rodriguez, M. (2007). "Relations among multiple peer influences, body dissatisfaction, eating disturbance, and self-esteem: A comparison of average weight, at risk of overweight, and overweight adolescent girls." *Journal of Pediatric Psychology*, 32(1), 24–29.

Thompson, L. (2016). *A Little Thing Called Life*. New York, NY: HarperCollins.

Tylka, T.L. & Sabik, N.J. (2010). "Integrating social comparison theory and self-esteem within objectification theory to predict women's disordered eating." *Sex Roles: A Journal of Research*, 63(1–2), 18–31.

van de Grift, T.C., Cohen-Kettenis, P.T., Steensma, T.D., Cuypere, G., *et al.* (2016a). "Body satisfaction and physical appearance in gender dysphoria." *Archives of Sexual Behavior*, 45(3), 575–585. doi:10.1007/s10508-015-0614-1.

van de Grift, T.C., Kreukels, B.P.C., Elfering, L., Özer, M., *et al.* (2016b). "Body image in transmen: Multidimensional measurement and the effects of mastectomy." *The Journal of Sexual Medicine*, 13(11), 1778–1786.

van der Kolk, B. (2015). *The Body Keeps the Score: Brain, Mind and Body in the Healing of Trauma*. New York, NY: Penguin Random House Books.

Watson, R.J., Veale, J.F., & Saewyc, E.M. (2017). "Disordered eating behaviors among transgender youth: Probability profiles from risk and protective factors." *The International Journal of Eating Disorders*, 50(5), 515–522.

Wertheim, E.H. & Paxton, S.J. (2011). "Body Image Development in Adolescent Girls." In T.F. Cash & L. Smolak (eds) *Body Image: A Handbook of Science and Prevention* (pp.76–84). New York, NY: The Guilford Press.

White Hughto, J.M., Reisner, S.L., & Pachankis, J.E. (2015). "Transgender stigma and health: A critical review of stigma determinants, mechanisms, and interventions." *Social Science & Medicine*, 147, 222–231.

Zosuls, K.M., Ruble, D.N., Tamis-Lemonda, C.S., Shrout, P.E., Bornstein, M.H., & Greulich F.K. (2009). "The acquisition of gender labels in infancy: Implications for gender-typed play." *Developmental Psychology*, 45(3), 688–701.

Zuba, A. & Warschburger, P. (2018). "Weight bias internalization across weight categories among school-aged children. Validation of the Weight Bias Internalization Scale for Children." *Body Image*, 25, 56–65.

Subject Index

Author Index